THE AMERICAN WEST
IN THE NINETEENTH CENTURY

255 Illustrations from "Harper's Weekly"
and Other Contemporary Sources

JOHN GRAFTON

DOVER PUBLICATIONS, INC.

New York

FRONTISPIECE: R. F. Zogbaum, *Harper's* specialist on military subjects, published this picture of "The Special Correspondent" in 1889. The accompanying article doesn't mention the time and place portrayed; if it was a self-portrait, the reticent Zogbaum didn't say so. However, as the artist spent a lot of time riding with the Cavalry in the West, it isn't too fanciful to see it as an idealized portrait of all the artist-correspondents who, in the days before photography made them obsolete, brought the events of Western history home for readers in the East. (*Harper's Weekly*, July 20, 1889; R. F. Zogbaum.)

Copyright © 1992 by Dover Publications, Inc.
All rights reserved under Pan American and International Copyright Conventions.

Published in Canada by General Publishing Company, Ltd., 30 Lesmill Road, Don Mills, Toronto, Ontario.
Published in the United Kingdom by Constable and Company, Ltd., 3 The Lanchesters, 162–164 Fulham Palace Road, London W6 9ER.

The American West in the Nineteenth Century: 255 Illustrations from "Harper's Weekly" and Other Contemporary Sources is a new work, first published by Dover Publications, Inc., in 1992.

DOVER *Pictorial Archive* SERIES

Manufactured in the United States of America
Dover Publications, Inc., 31 East 2nd Street, Mineola, N.Y. 11501

Library of Congress Cataloging-in-Publication Data

The American West in the nineteenth century : 255 illustrations from "Harper's weekly" and other contemporary sources / by John Grafton.
       p.   cm.
   Includes index.
   ISBN 0-486-27304-0 (pbk.)
   1. West (U.S.)—Pictorial works. 2. West (U.S.)—History—Pictorial works. I. Grafton, John.
F591.A413 1992
978'.02—dc20   92-15667
                                                                        CIP

Contents

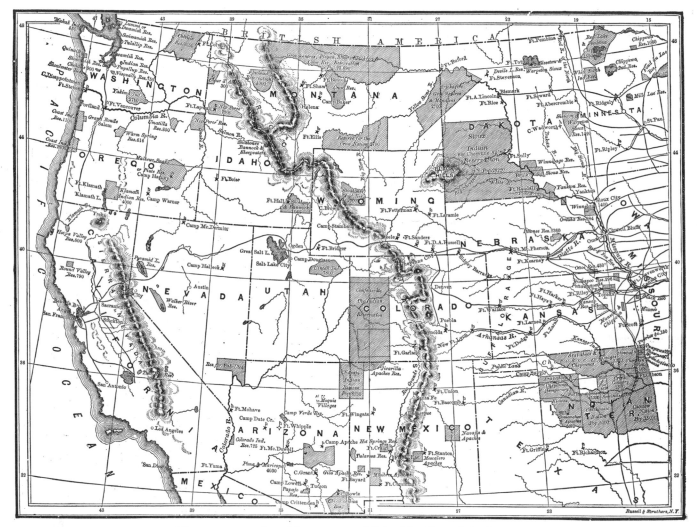

The map reproduced here was published by *Harper's* in August 1874 at the time of Custer's exploring expedition to the Black Hills. It was designed to show the main Indian reservations and military posts in the West at that time. (*Harper's Weekly*, August 22, 1874.)

Introduction

IN 1854 THERE WERE SIX American states established west of the Mississippi River—Iowa, Missouri, Arkansas, Louisiana, Texas and California. Three more would soon be added—Minnesota in 1858, Oregon in 1859 and Kansas in 1861. The remaining lands of the American West were organized into eight territories of varying sizes—Washington, Dakota, Nebraska, Colorado, Utah, Nevada, New Mexico and the Indian Territory (present-day Oklahoma). The Mormons had settled in the Great Salt Lake area in the 1840s; the Gold Rush had brought thousands across the continent to California from 1849 on; and the Oregon Trail had led tens of thousands more to the fertile valleys of the Pacific Northwest at roughly the same time. The vast interior of the country was still, however, largely unpopulated and little known.

In less than four decades all of this would be changed. The buffalo would be practically exterminated; the search for gold and silver would bring fortune seekers to every corner of the West, no matter how unpromising and inaccessible; a network of railroads would cross the continent in every direction; and millions of Texas cattle and legions of Eastern farmers would overrun the northern plains, control of which would be, painfully but completely, wrested from the Indians. In the 1840s the explorer John Charles Frémont traveled over vast areas of the West that had remained unchanged in the four decades since Lewis and Clark had set out for the Pacific in 1803. That experience would not be available to any traveler 40 years after Frémont.

As the four decades between 1850 and 1890 were crucial ones in the development of the modern American West, we are fortunate in having some remarkable pictorial sources to go to for glimpses of what these vast changes looked like. That this record was created at that time and place is owed to the foresight of a few alert publishers, particularly the Harper brothers and Frank Leslie.

Two brothers, John and James Harper, established their first small printing business on New York's Dover Street in 1817. Two more brothers, Wesley and Fletcher, later joined them, and the firm's name was changed to Harper & Brothers in 1833. Their first magazine, the small-format *Harper's New Monthly Magazine*, was inaugurated in 1850. Seven years later the first issue of *Harper's Weekly* rolled off their active presses. For a nickel, each week readers got 16 folio pages filled with the news of the world. More importantly, they saw pictures, reproduced through the medium of wood engraving, of everything imaginable: African natives, English cathedrals, rare snakes and birds, scientific inventions, portraits of the famous and the notable, scenes of everyday life, political cartoons and, above all, the events of the day.

Harper's Weekly came of age during the Civil War. With the services of a unique group of artists that included Winslow Homer and a score of others who are less well remembered today, the newspaper created a unique and compelling pictorial record of each week's events. When the war ended, *Harper's Weekly* went right on covering every big story that came its way. One of the biggest in the following decades was what was happening in the American West. The Harper brothers sent many of their best artists out West: beginning with Theodore R. Davis and Alfred R. Waud right after the Civil War, continuing with Paul Frenzeny and Jules Tavernier in the early 1870s, concluding with military correspondent R. F. Zogbaum during the height of the Indian Wars, and Frederic Remington himself during the campaign against Geronimo in the 1880s. A selection from the hundreds of Western pictures *Harper's* published before the end of the century is reproduced on many of the pages that follow.

Frank Leslie was born in England in 1821 and worked as a wood engraver on the staff of *The Illustrated London News* in the 1840s. After emigrating to America, he worked for a time on *Gleason's Pictorial*, published in Boston. In 1853 he came to New York to head the engraving department of a new publication, the *Illustrated News*, which issued its first number on January 1, 1853. Shortly he was on his own, and the first issue of his most important publication, *Frank Leslie's Illustrated Newspaper*, came out on December 15, 1855.

Like his rivals at *Harper's*, Leslie commissioned artists to record the campaigns of the Civil War. Like them, he turned part of his attention toward the West in the decades after the war. In the later 1870s Leslie took a trainload of prominent Easterners on a cross-country tour. The transcontinental railroad was still an innovation, and the reports of this excursion no doubt boosted circulation. Leslie didn't forget to bring some of his artists along. Happily for students of Western mining, the tour rolled into Virginia City just when activity on Nevada's Comstock Lode was at its height.

Leslie was an entrepreneur in the nineteenth-century mode. He started dozens of publications, made and lost fortunes, was always ready to seize the publishing moment. His editorial slant was a little more unbuttoned and raffish than that of *Harper's*, but, true to his origins as a wood engraver, he had an eye for quality and craftsmanship.

It is pointless today to lament the end of the wood-engraving era, but surely something was lost at the end of the nineteenth century when illustrated periodicals began to replace crisp wood engravings with muddy halftone reproductions of photographs. It was possible to take a good photograph long before it was possible to reproduce one effectively for mass circulation. In the following pages, readers will notice that there was something of a transitional phase when the weeklies occasionally created wood engravings based on photographs rather than sketches. By the end of the century the illustrated weeklies were just about totally committed to photographs. The wood-engraving era passed into history.

Any writer who discusses the role of the great illustrated weeklies in the history of Western art will be indebted to the late Prof. Robert Taft of the University of Kansas. Taft's pioneering 1953 book, *Artists and Illustrators of the Old West*, opened up this subject to serious exploration. A chemist by profession, Taft spent decades of his spare time tracking down biographical information on the artists, famous and unknown, whose work is reproduced on these pages. In his book, Taft wrote that one of the things that aroused his interest in the subject was the illustration reproduced on page 66 of the present volume. The haunting desolation of the busted Kansas town stayed in his mind for years, stimulating him to find out something of its history, and the history of the artists who recorded its image. From there it was a short leap to extend his research to the many other artists reproduced here, men whose work still has the power to fascinate us.

JOHN GRAFTON

Princeton, New Jersey
March 1992

NOTE: Some of the illustrations in the present volume are details from wood engravings, rather than the entire original engravings.

A buffalo skinner with the hide of a dead animal. As buffalo hunting evolved into a business in the 1870s, most skinners worked for hunters at a fixed wage—$30 to $50 a month—and occasionally a share of the profits. Often skinners worked in pairs. Two experienced skinners could remove a hide weighing 80 to 100 pounds in five minutes. Hides were always removed the day the buffalo was shot. Fresh hides were spread out in the sun hair-side down and pegged to the ground to dry. The drying process took three to five days and reduced the weight of the hide by half. Arsenic or some other poison was poured over the hide to kill insects. (*Harper's Weekly*, December 12, 1874; Frenzeny and Tavernier.)

Hunting: The Death of the Buffalo

EXCEPT FOR A FEW EXPLORERS like Lewis and Clark and Zebulon Pike, who journeyed West for the government in the early years of the nineteenth century, the region was first explored, and first exploited, by hunters and fur trappers. Other than Indians, the first to penetrate many remote areas were the legendary mountain men and the pioneer entrepreneurs with whom they traded their pelts at the annual Rocky Mountain rendezvous in the 1820s and 1830s. The knowledge of Western terrain and trails through the wilderness, which soldiers, pioneers, miners and railroad builders would sorely need later on, owed much to trailblazing mountain men like Jedediah Strong Smith, the first white man to travel overland from the Rockies to California, and Joseph Reddeford Walker, who investigated the San Joaquin Valley route around the southern end of the Sierra Nevada and the Humboldt River route between the Sierra and Salt Lake.

The French and English had conducted the fur trade in North America, from the Great Lakes to the Pacific Northwest, for over a century before the American Revolution. The British Hudson's Bay Company was the leading player in this arena until John Jacob Astor invaded Oregon by sea in 1811 and established his competing Pacific Fur Company. In addition to beaver, the fur companies in the Pacific Northwest did a thriving trade in sea-otter pelts, which they traded mostly in China. So devastating were the effects of the otter trade that even today there are only a few thousand of these endangered animals in the area where they once roamed by the millions.

For the great mountain men in the early years of the nineteenth century, the life of the beaver trapper was idyllic though demanding. Beaver were hunted with underwater traps from each year's spring thaw until midsummer, when the animals molted, and then again in the autumn until the creeks and rivers froze. Throughout the entire West in those years there were never more than several hundred active trappers. A good year for a trapper saw him take 300 to 400 beaver pelts; Smith once took 668 in one year, which is generally considered the unofficial record. The pelts could be traded at the annual rendezvous for whatever the trapper needed to maintain himself for another year. A St. Louis entrepreneur, William Henry Ashley, conceived the idea of the annual fur trappers' rendezvous in the early 1820s. For over a decade thereafter the trappers came together once each year for days and nights of feasting, drinking, gambling and general mayhem while also conducting business. Ashley and his partners took the pelts back to Missouri where they brought $3 to $6 each.

The system worked well as long as the beaver trade flourished. The era of the mountain men began to fade into history primarily because this trade died rather suddenly around 1840. First, the beaver became harder to find. After years of increasingly serious trapping, the animals, though by no means endangered, weren't as plentiful or as accessible as they had been. More importantly, the beaver hat went out of fashion in the East. No longer so highly prized, the beaver pelt that had brought $6 a few years earlier now was worth no more than $1. The wise trappers, including many renowned mountain men, quickly went on to other lines of work.

The decimation of the beaver foreshadowed the greatest slaughter of animals in human history—the attack on the American buffalo in the 1870s and early 1880s. Possibly 75 million buffalo occupied North America before the first Europeans arrived, and before the Plains Indians acquired horses early in the eighteenth century. Commercial hunting of the buffalo began early in the nineteenth century. At first it was limited to the winter months, when the animals' coats were fullest, to fill the heavy Eastern demand for buffalo robes. In those decades perhaps 100,000 robes were shipped East each year, and the herds remained huge. Many travelers in the first half of the nineteenth century came across herds that covered 50 or more square miles. Major Richard Irving Dodge saw a herd in Kansas in 1871 that took five days to pass. A few years earlier, the steamboat *Stockade* had been left dead in the water for hours on the upper Missouri while a huge herd crossed the river. At the end of the Civil War there were probably still 20 million buffalo left.

The real slaughter began around 1870, spurred by the development of methods of manufacturing commercial leather from buffalo hides. As the leather industry in the East boomed, the demand for hides multiplied. Buffalo could be killed for hides at any time of year. The new Western railroads also played a part in the great buffalo hunt. The animals were killed to provide food for the workers who built the railroads, and by passengers stopping for a moment of sport shooting on the plains. More importantly, the railroads brought an army of professional hunters West, and facilitated the shipment East of great quantities of hides. Beginning in Kansas around 1870–71, continuing in Texas over the middle years of the decade, and ending after 1880 on the northern plains, just a few thousand hunters wiped out the herds.

Dodge City, Kansas, was one of the centers of the buffalo-hide industry early in the 1870s. In the winter of 1872–73, one Dodge City firm shipped 200,000 hides East on the Santa Fe Railroad. Once the hides were disposed of, the bones were also often marketed. Dried buffalo bones were worth about $8 a ton in the 1870s and 1880s when sold to fertilizer manufacturers. It took a hundred carcasses to produce a ton of dried bones. Thousands of tons rolled out of Dodge during the buffalo-hunting era. After several years, so many hunters were killing so many animals that hides that had brought $3 or $4 were barely worth a dollar on the market. The hunters just killed more to make up the difference. It was observed at the time by many in the East that the Plains Indians would surely be driven to violence against the white man and eventually destroyed by the wasteful slaughter of the buffalo. Some saw this as a desirable result, and, in any case, a few editorials couldn't stop the killing.

By the end of the 1880s there were only a few hundred buffalo left in North America. (Through the efforts of conservationists there are today more than 10,000 on federal game preserves.) The role played by the slaughter of the buffalo in Western history can hardly be overemphasized. Destruction of the herds cleared the plains for the farmers and the ranchers. It also precipitated the final phases of the struggle between the Army and the many tribes of Plains Indians whose traditional way of life had always depended totally on the buffalo. The interconnected developments of the coming of the railroads and the destruction of the buffalo herds signified more than anything else the imminent closing of the American frontier.

2   Hunting: The Death of the Buffalo

OPPOSITE, TOP: In order to leave no trail, a solitary Western hunter leads his horse through a stream that skirts a barely visible Indian village in the upper right-hand corner. *Harper's* published this sketch in 1876, during the period when the final conflict with the Indians on the northern plains was at its height. (*Harper's Weekly*, September 9, 1876; W. M. Cary.) OPPOSITE, BOTTOM: Toward the end of the century, when the beaver trapper and the buffalo hunter were no longer to be found in the Western states, Frederic Remington published this sketch of a convoy of crude wagons coming down from a season's hunting and trapping in the most inaccessible reaches of the Canadian Rockies. These French-Indian trappers and their equipment recall a period in Western history that had by then all but vanished, but men like these were still able to make a living hunting and trapping in the far north for mink, deer, otter, sable, beaver, bear and even now and then a buffalo. (*Harper's Weekly*, August 25, 1888; Frederic Remington.) ABOVE: Fur traders heading downstream are ambushed by Indians on the Missouri River. From the earliest days of Western exploration, the Missouri was the route to the rich fur-trapping lands of the Northwest. To bring their pelts to market, fur traders on the upper Missouri waited through the winter to take advantage of swift currents following the spring thaw. They could then make the 2,400-mile journey to St. Louis from the Montana Territory in about two weeks in these simple boats with their unusual bow-mounted oars for maneuverability. Pelts were wrapped for the trip in deerskin-covered bales weighing up to 100 pounds each. Artist W. M. Cary knew the hazards of the upper Missouri from firsthand experience. In 1868, the year in which he drew this picture, Cary was a passenger on a Missouri steamboat that exploded and sank. Later, he was captured by Crow Indians while traveling overland from Fort Union to Fort Benton. Released through the intervention of a fur-company official known to the Indians, he returned to New York for a long and prolific career as an illustrator and painter. (*Harper's Weekly*, May 23, 1868; W. M. Cary.)

4   *Hunting: The Death of the Buffalo*

OPPOSITE: An imaginative illustration of an Indian signaling to his sheltered village below that a buffalo herd is in sight. To the Indians on the Western plains, the buffalo was essential. Buffalo meat was the staple of their diet. Meat that wasn't eaten fresh was preserved by being dried in the sun or over a low fire, then pounded into a mass, combined with layers of melted buffalo fat and packed into bags made of buffalo skin. This preserved meat, called pemmican, would remain edible for years. The hides were used for shelter and blankets. The bones were fashioned into weapons, tools, ornaments and toys. Sinews were used for bowstrings. Where no other fuel was available, dried buffalo dung was burned for cooking and for heat. By 1873 the herds in Kansas were largely played out, and the white buffalo hunters moved to Texas. There they met some resistance. In June 1874 a combined force of Comanche, Cheyenne and Kiowa braves attacked a buffalo hunters' camp at Adobe Walls, 150 miles southwest of Dodge. The hunters were outnumbered, but the range and accuracy of their Sharps rifles, equipped with telescopic sights, kept the Indians at bay, and the battle ended indecisively. The Cavalry eventually forced the Indians back to their reservations, and the buffalo hunting went on. By the end of the decade, the Texas herds were wiped out, and the hunters moved on to Montana, the Dakota Territory and Wyoming. Within four or five years the northern herds were gone as well. (*Harper's Weekly*, March 22, 1873; W. M. Cary.) ABOVE: A ring of mature buffalo bulls protecting their herd from a pack of wolves. Wolves followed the buffalo herds, picking off any young, old or sick animals that became separated from the others. Wolves were no match for mature, healthy bulls, who killed them easily, flipping them in the air with their horns and then trampling them with their hooves. (*Harper's Weekly*, August 5, 1871; W. M. Cary.)

OPPOSITE, TOP: A mounted hunter shooting a buffalo with a revolver. This 1870 engraving depicts the sort of hunting that had been done earlier in the century. When buffalo hunting became commercialized, hunters found they could kill more efficiently shooting with rifles from a kneeling or prone position. (*Appleton's Journal*, 1870; Felix O. C. Darley.) OPPOSITE, BOTTOM: Indians attacking a herd of buffalo in the Missouri River. Some of the Indians hunted with bows and arrows from small boats while others waited on the bank to finish off wounded animals. Some found it easy to kill the largely defenseless buffaloes with knives in midstream; they then pulled the dead animals back to shore by their tails. (*Harper's Weekly*, May 16, 1874; W. M. Cary.) ABOVE: A professional buffalo hunter finishing off a wounded animal in

Montana in the 1880s. Professional hunters were masters of their craft, able to kill from a distance of 200 to 300 yards by shooting a buffalo through the lungs, after which the animal would pump blood through its nostrils and drop dead where it stood. A bull shot through the heart might run hundreds of yards and take the rest of the herd with him. Many hunters killed 3,000 to 5,000 in a single year, and 100 to 200 at a single stand was common. A hunter named Wright Moar estimated that he had killed 20,500 buffalo in seven years. Another named Brick Bond killed 5,855 between October and December 1871, keeping five skinners busy until he went deaf from the sound of his own guns. (*The Illustrated London News*, October 23, 1886; R. Caton Woodville.)

8 Hunting: The Death of the Buffalo

OPPOSITE, TOP: A buffalo hunter's camp in western Kansas. Armed with long-range weapons such as the Sharps .45-caliber rifle, which at 15 pounds was too heavy to be used on horseback, hunters often used the forked branch of a tree to steady their rifle barrels. They tried to kill quickly and surely, leaving the carcasses close together for their skinners, who followed with the sort of wagons seen here. There was little hunters could do with the meat they didn't eat themselves. Buffalo tongues, a delicacy, brought 25 cents in the 1870s. Buffalo meat, however, was so plentiful it was hardly worth a penny a pound, and was left on the plains to rot. (*The Graphic*, February 10, 1877; S. E. Waller.) OPPOSITE, BOTTOM: A herd of buffalo attacked by the passengers and crew of a Kansas–Pacific train between Ellis, Kansas, and Kit Carson, Colorado, in 1871. In 1875 the Kansas–Pacific bowed to popular and editorial pressure from the East, and stopped allowing its passengers to shoot buffalo and other game from its trains, a practice it had at first encouraged to attract tourists. (*Frank Leslie's Illustrated Newspaper*, June 3, 1871; Albert Berghaus, from a sketch by Henry Worrall.) ABOVE: There was hunting in the West before the buffalo hunters came, and hunters remained after the buffalo were gone. This sketch of a deer hunter's shack in the Rocky Mountains was published even as the frontier was closing. By the early 1880s the war against the buffalo was over. The buffalo hunters, like the beaver trappers before them, moved on to other professions. Some of the West's famous peace officers, men like Wyatt Earp, Pat Garrett and Bat Masterson, all had an early fling at buffalo hunting. The most famous hunter of them all was William F. (Buffalo Bill) Cody. He went from a brief career as a hunter supplying buffalo meat to railroad workers to become the legendary showman of the American West. (*Harper's Weekly*, April 19, 1890; Charles Graham.)

A party of gold prospectors who died of starvation in New Mexico's Sierra Madre Mountains. This specific incident may have been apocryphal, but the dangers faced by those searching the mountains of the West for gold and silver in the nineteenth century were real enough—accidents in remote areas, bad weather, hostile Indians, wild animals, little food or water in some locations, impure water and rampant disease in others. It would be impossible to calculate the number of lives lost to the search for precious metals in the West in the nineteenth century, but it was certainly many thousands. (*Frank Leslie's Illustrated Newspaper*, October 11, 1884.)

The Gold Rush and the Mining Frontier

THE COURSE OF WESTERN history was changed forever on January 24, 1848, when millwright James Wilson Marshall discovered gold at Sutter's Mill on the South Fork of the American River at Coloma, 45 miles northeast of Sacramento. Explorers, trappers and fur traders had been active on the Pacific coast for decades. The first struggling wagon trains of settlers had crossed the Rockies and the Sierra to Oregon and California in the early 1840s. In a few months during 1849 alone, however, the California Gold Rush brought many thousands more across the continent than had made the trip during the 45 years since Lewis and Clark had set out for the Pacific.

The Gold Rush did not start immediately following Marshall's discovery. Reports of gold were treated skeptically at first, but by the end of May 1848 a local rush was on with a few hundred miners in the field. Midsummer saw 3,000 at the diggings; there were perhaps twice that many by the end of the year. Almost all of these hopeful gold seekers of 1848 came to the Mother Lode country from somewhere else in California. A large number were deserting soldiers and sailors.

In the East, as 1848 wore on, the news of gold in California stirred little attention. On September 14 a prominent Eastern newspaper, the *Philadelphia North American and United States Gazette,* published an account of gold excitement in California that had been sent to them by the Rev. Walter Colton of Monterey. "The farmers have thrown aside their plows," Colton wrote, "the lawyers their briefs, the doctors their pills, the priests their prayer books, and all are now digging gold." The Eastern states remained unconvinced. In June 1848, however, the military governor of California, Col. Richard B. Mason, had toured the diggings and had sent back a report to the Secretary of War. On December 5, 1848, President James Polk was able to use it as the basis of an enthusiastic account of California's gold in his opening message to the second session of the Thirtieth Congress. When Polk's remarks were made public, the Gold Rush was on.

A hundred thousand Easterners set out for California in 1849, approximately half by land and half by sea. By sea, travelers had two options. They could sail around Cape Horn and on up the western coasts of South and North America to San Francisco, or they could sail south to Panama from an Eastern port, then journey across the isthmus by land to Panama City and pick up another ship there for the trip north. Either way was expensive, with passage costing $400 to $1,000 depending on accommodations, and either journey could be slow and dangerous.

The Cape Horn route took from four to six months; the Panama route shortened the distance, but Panama was an expensive place to stay during the wait while booking passage north. Travelers also faced exposure to a variety of serious tropical diseases on the overland portion of their trip. The demand for passage to California was so great that some unseaworthy ships were pressed into service on both coasts, with predictably disastrous results. Still, some 700 ships arrived in San Francisco during 1849 bringing 45,000 or more hopeful forty-niners.

Overland, forty-niners came from all directions—from Mexico, from the American South via the Santa Fe Trail and, principally, from the East on the traditional Oregon/California Trail to the Rockies, South Pass and over the desert to the Sierra. They had it no easier by land than they did by sea. The spring of 1849 was unusually wet along the Mississippi, making it difficult for wagon trains to get started. Later that spring and summer, a cholera epidemic swept across the overland trails, killing perhaps one in ten. In 1849 as many as 5,000 overland "argonauts," as they had come to call themselves, were buried east of South Pass.

Those who reached the California mining camps found a reality somewhat different from what the glowing reports had led them to expect. They found back-breaking work in cold mountain streams, gold that proved elusive, poor food, rampant disease and incredibly high prices. They also found a violent, lawless society where the peaceful were at the mercy of criminals on the one hand and occasionally misguided vigilantes on the other. Many died, many went back where they came from and many stayed to work for years in poverty while a few did indeed strike it very rich. In the first four years of the Gold Rush, when gold was valued at $16 an ounce, $200 million worth was taken out of the ground in California, with 1852 the peak year at $81 million. By the end of the 1850s the total yield was about $600 million, but the days of placer mining—finding gold by sifting through the dirt and rocks of riverbeds—were coming to an end. Hundreds of millions of dollars' worth of precious metals remained to be mined in California, but not by the simple techniques of the lonely prospector panning for gold. With placer deposits exhausted, the mining future belonged to capitalists who could invest in the equipment needed to find and extract gold from quartz deposits deep below the earth's surface. The same progression would repeat itself across the West wherever gold was discovered.

The mining frontier moved east from California in the decades after the Gold Rush. Gold was found in the Pike's Peak region in 1859, sparking another rush from the East. Denver became the center of a large Rocky Mountain mining region in which many towns went through the familiar boom-and-bust cycle. At about the same time, valuable discoveries were made in the Washoe Range, about 20 miles south of the present city of Reno, Nevada. This was the Comstock Lode, named after one of the many colorful personalities in at the beginning. Its dual centers, Virginia City and Gold Hill, flourished as the quintessential raucous and rowdy Western mining towns. Those who were there were wise to enjoy it while it lasted. Before the end of the century, even the mighty Comstock was played out. In the 1870s rich strikes brought miners to the Black Hills in the Dakota Territory. While the Army and the federal government maneuvered the Sioux off land granted them before gold had been discovered there, legions scoured the area looking for that one big strike. In 1875 a prospector named Moses Manuel found the body of ore that in subsequent decades would be developed into one of the richest gold mines ever found on earth. South Dakota's Homestake Mine, still active today, has yielded well over $1 billion worth of gold.

Innumerable other areas throughout the West saw rich strikes in the last decades of the century. The pattern became familiar. Ore samples would be tested, claims would be recorded, mines would be dug, stage lines would be established and railroads planned and sometimes built. The last great gold rush sent thousands to the Klondike River in Canada's Yukon Territory as the century was drawing to a close. Today, the meaning of this massive, 50-year treasure hunt lies less in the value of the precious metals taken out of the ground than in its effect on Western history. The Gold Rush and subsequent mineral strikes brought Americans and immigrants West when the land was empty and ready to be claimed. While a few made fortunes at it, thousands stayed after the excitement was over to farm, to ranch and to build the permanent towns and cities. Even those who went home disappointed had at least "seen the elephant"—in the expression of the day—and had been a part of one of the greatest of American adventures.

ABOVE, TOP: San Francisco in January 1850. This engraving was made from a daguerreotype taken two years after gold was discovered and about one year after the Gold Rush began. In 1849 the population of San Francisco, the gateway to California's mining region, rose from 3,000 to 20,000. Ships carrying new immigrants from all over the world docked almost daily. Housing was scarce. A bunk in a huge dormitory might cost $20 a week, while a regular hotel room could bring $250. Some solved the housing problem by living on ships whose crews had abandoned them to dig for gold. Others pitched tents wherever they could. San Francisco in the era of the Barbary Coast was a place unlike any other in American history. Goods were scarce, so prices rose constantly. Eggs might cost $1 each, ordinary meals $5, prices that would have been absurd in New York or Chicago in the 1850s. Labor was so scarce that laundry was sometimes sent to China or Hawaii. While the streets up and down the steep hills of the city were still unpaved quagmires of mud much of the year, theaters, opera houses, circuses and saloons sprang up regularly. Lola Montez and Edwin Booth and a host of other luminaries per-

formed there. There was so much gold passing through that hundreds of gambling establishments crowded the city, their numbers rivaled only by the houses of prostitution. (*The Illustrated London News*, October 19, 1850.) LEFT: Blay Place, a commercial San Francisco street, in 1850. With goods of all kinds scarce, but gold to buy them plentiful, an astute merchant in San Francisco during the Gold Rush could make a fortune more easily than all but the luckiest prospectors. (*The Illustrated London News*, October 19, 1850.) OPPOSITE, TOP: A famous California murder, the shooting of James King by James P. Casey in 1856. This was a crucial event in the history of San Francisco's Vigilance Committees. Aroused by arson and looting during the series of six fires that devastated San Francisco during the first years of the Gold Rush, and by the inability of the authorities to deal with the city's large and ever-growing criminal population, the 1851 Vigilance Committee came into being. It was comprised of over 600 members, primarily bankers, businessmen and shopkeepers. During 1851 the Committee hanged four lawbreakers, whipped one, deported 20, turned 15 over to the regular authorities and released 41 after trial. The net result was a decline in violent crimes, and later that year the Committee disbanded. The Committee was remarkable in that its members included some of the most prominent citizens of the city, and it carried out its actions with no attempt at secrecy. In the event illustrated here, James P. Casey, a city politician and candidate for the post of City Supervisor, shot James King, the reforming editor of the *Evening Bulletin*, because King had written, truthfully, that Casey was a former convict and inmate of a New York State penitentiary. Six days after the shooting, King died, and the call went out to form a new Vigilance Committee. The new Committee seized Casey and brought him to its headquarters. He was convicted, and hanged on May 22, 1856. (*Frank Leslie's Illustrated Newspaper*, July 19, 1856.) OPPOSITE, BOTTOM: The July 29 hanging of two murderers, Joseph Hetherington and Philander Brace, by the 1856 Committee. A crowd of several thousand turned out to witness this event. Shortly after this execution, the 1856 Committee disbanded. Hardly anywhere else in the West would vigilantes earn the reputation for fairness that has been history's judgment on the San Francisco Committees. (*Frank Leslie's Illustrated Newspaper*, September 13, 1856.)

ABOVE, LEFT: A contemporary woodcut of Sutter's Mill at Coloma on the South Fork of the American River. It was here that on January 24, 1848, millwright James Wilson Marshall discovered California's gold. The Swiss soldier of fortune Johann Augustus Sutter had arrived in California in the late 1830s. Securing a land grant of 48,818 acres from the Mexican authorities, he established his wooden, fortress-like headquarters, which he named New Helvetia, at the junction of the Sacramento and American Rivers, near the site of the present city of Sacramento. Sutter developed his land into a huge self-contained farming and ranching operation, including his own gristmill, tannery and distillery. Needing timber for building, he hired Marshall to build the sawmill at Coloma, 45 miles northeast of New Helvetia. Ironically, the discovery of gold at the new sawmill spelled ruin rather than prosperity for Sutter. Within two years, his land was overrun by thousands of prospectors. Sutter, who died a poor man in 1880, spent the rest of his life trying, unsuccessfully, to obtain compensation from the American government for his ruined fortunes. (Henry Howe: *Historical Collections of the Great West*, 1851.) ABOVE, RIGHT: An early woodcut of a group of prospectors during the first years of the Gold Rush. Created by volcanic activity thousands of years earlier, California's placer gold deposits (the word "placer" derives from a Spanish word for a sandbank) had gradually been washed down the mountainsides by the hundreds of rivers and creeks that run through the Sierra foothills. Thus it was to the riverbeds and creeks that prospectors went to search for gold. Where there was no water, there was no gold. The first prospectors simply dug visible pieces of gold out of rocky crevasses with hunting knives. The gold that could be obtained this way was soon exhausted, and more sophisticated methods of washing dirt for gold were then called for. (Henry Howe: *Historical Collections of the Great West*, 1851.) OPPOSITE, TOP: The great Sacramento fire of November 2, 1852. This fire destroyed most of the town, including every public building except the courthouse and the Presbyterian church. Founded in 1848, Sacramento's crucial position at the junction of the Sacramento and American Rivers, 75 miles northeast of San Francisco, made it the central point of shipment by steamboat for men and goods to and from the mining district in the Sierra foothills. From Sacramento, stage lines fanned out in all directions to the mining camps. Sacramento was ravaged by several large fires and some impressive floods in its early years. Like San Francisco, it quickly rebuilt itself after every disaster, and grew up with the Gold Rush to become the state capital in 1854. In the following decade the city was selected as the Western terminus of the first transcontinental railroad. (*Illustrated News*, January 1, 1853.) OPPOSITE, BOTTOM: A bustling Sacramento street scene in 1878. With the transcontinental railroad completed and the city's position as state capital established, Sacramento continued to prosper as an agricultural center long after the Gold Rush. (*Frank Leslie's Illustrated Newspaper*, May 4, 1878.)

LEFT: A California prospector on his way to a mining camp with all the supplies needed for a long stretch in the open. Thousands of gold-mining camps sprang up in 1848 and the following years along the western slopes of the Sierra foothills. Eventually California's Mother Lode country covered 200 miles between Rich Bar on the North Fork of the Feather River and Mormon Bar on the Mariposa River. (*Illustrated News*, February 5, 1853.) BELOW: Washing for gold in the Sierra foothills. The prospector's basic tool for extracting gold from the sand and dirt of the riverbeds was a tin or iron pan. The prospector scooped up a panful of dirt from the riverbed, and through skillful manipulation of the pan, washed the lighter pebbles and sand over the side while picking off worthless rocks and gravel. As he did this, the heavier gold-bearing sand settled to the bottom of the pan. It was tiring work, usually involving standing in the river for hours on end; each panful might yield only a few small particles of gold, or nothing at all. A tireless worker could wash perhaps 50 panfuls a day. Gradually, prospectors turned to using cradles to wash dirt faster. Cradles were wooden boxes three or four feet long set on rockers. Earth and water were dumped into the cradle; as the cradle was rocked, rocks and pebbles were picked out by hand while the water washed the dirt and sand out through a sieve at one end. The heavier gold-bearing sand settled to the bottom where it was caught and held by strips of wood. The final step was to wash this gold-bearing sand with a pan. Extended cradles, called Long Toms, quickly came into use. Finally, even longer wooden sluices—up to 30 feet—improved on the efficiency of the Long Tom. In this view, the man kneeling in the left foreground is working with a small cradle-like device while behind him others are shoveling dirt into longer sluices. (S. Bowles: *Across the Continent*, 1853.)

More than 20 prospectors may be found in this seemingly quiet scene drawn by J. D. Borthwick for *The Illustrated London News* in 1851. Borthwick was an English artist who went to California as a prospector when the Gold Rush began, but soon abandoned the miner's life to practice his own profession. He did a lively business drawing portraits of successful prospectors, who sent them back East to friends and families. The scene depicted here is at Kanoha Bar, 18 miles down the South Fork of the American River from Coloma. A company of 15 miners who employed 15 hired hands spent $3,500 and two months building this long wooden flume to divert the river during the summer months. This allowed them to use the water in the most efficient way possible for washing dirt, and gave them access to the riverbed, where they hoped plentiful deposits of gold would be found. Several long sluices for washing gold are seen branching off from the flume. Borthwick reported that when he drew this sketch, the company had already found enough gold to repay their investment, and hoped to show a profit before the winter rainy season shut them down. If the claim was not exhausted by then, the flume could be dismantled and reassembled in the spring. In an area where trees were scarce, the lumber to build this flume had been too expensive ($130 for each thousand board feet) to waste. Many fortunes were made in Western mining areas by those who supplied lumber to miners. Even greater fortunes were made by those who, not prospectors themselves, diverted rivers and streams to supply water where it was needed to work promising claims. By the end of the 1850s hundreds of miles of ditches, canals and wooden flumes like this one had been built throughout the Mother Lode country at a cost of millions of dollars, investments that were sometimes amply repaid. (*The Illustrated London News*, January 24, 1852; J. D. Borthwick.)

OPPOSITE, TOP: A Chinese mining camp in California in the 1850s. The Chinese entered California by the thousands in the decade after gold was discovered. Keeping primarily to themselves, Chinese prospectors were objects of curiosity to the forty-niners from the Eastern states. They were also often victims of discrimination and violence in the never-ending competition for the most desirable claims. Lacking any recourse, Chinese prospectors were often relegated to working over claims that others had given up as played out, but the painstaking thoroughness with which they worked generally enabled them still to reap modest rewards. (*Harper's Weekly*, October 3, 1857; J. D. Borthwick.) OPPOSITE, MIDDLE: Prospectors in the Mother Lode country, cooking their evening meal. Life in the mining camps was hardly idyllic. Working all day in cold mountain streams and sleeping on the cold, damp ground in areas where food was scarce, sewage disposal haphazard, water often impure and doctors almost unknown, left the forty-niners and their followers susceptible to pneumonia, cholera, scurvy, typhoid fever, meningitis, rheumatic fever and dysentery. (Those who came via Panama could add malaria and yellow fever to this catalogue.) Everything they needed was so expensive that it was widely believed that it was necessary to find an ounce of gold a day just to pay expenses and show a small profit. This was not easy to do, and many left in discouragement. Others were periodically buoyed up by reports, often apocryphal, of the lucky few who had found lumps of solid gold weighing up to 25 pounds. (*Harper's Weekly*, October 3, 1857; J. D. Borthwick.) OPPOSITE, BOTTOM: A typical mining-camp entertainment, a men-only square dance. Women were scarce in the Sierra foothills in the 1850s. (*Harper's Weekly*, October 3, 1857; J. D. Borthwick.) ABOVE: A mining-camp gambling hall. Gambling was the downfall of many prospectors who worked for weeks or months to make a small stake, only to lose it in a second on the turn of a card or a roll of the dice. Gamblers followed the mining camps, as they later followed the cowboys and the railroad builders, waiting to play for the rewards of the prospector's work. (*Harper's Weekly*, October 3, 1857; J. D. Borthwick.)

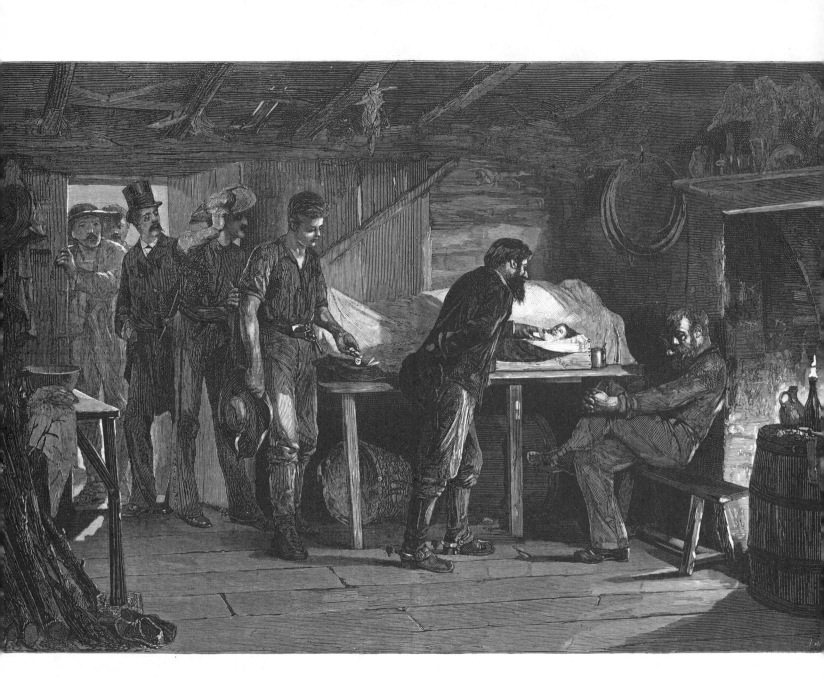

ABOVE: The writer who brought the Gold Rush home to America in the nineteenth century was Bret Harte. Harte arrived in San Francisco not long after the Gold Rush began. He spent several years there before leaving for England, where he lived for the rest of his life. In hundreds of stories and poems, Harte recreated, imaginatively and sentimentally, the world of the forty-niners. One of his most famous stories was "The Luck of Roaring Camp." The central incident of the story is illustrated here—a rustic miner's cabin into which are filing the varied characters of Roaring Camp, all coming to see the baby of a prostitute who had died in childbirth. (*Harper's Weekly*, May 7, 1881; from a painting by Henry Bacon.) OPPOSITE, TOP: The interior of a prospector's cabin in the early years of the Gold Rush.

As the 1850s wore on, surface deposits of gold in the Mother Lode country were gradually played out, and the mining history of California passed into a new, less carefree, phase. Placer mining gave way to more sophisticated techniques involving tunneling into the ground to bring gold-bearing ore to the surface, and hydraulic mining, in which hillsides were swept away with the spray from powerful hoses to provide literally mountains of earth to be washed by large sluices. The solitary prospector out for the strike of a lifetime moved on to other areas, or found another line of work. Those who stayed became the employees of the mining industry, far removed from the romantic image of the self-reliant argonaut of 1849. (*Illustrated News*, February 19, 1853.)

RIGHT: A graphic reminder of the lawlessness and violence that marked the Gold Rush years: a poster advertising the exhibition of the head of the legendary California bandit Joaquín Murieta. In 1853 the California legislature became concerned about crimes being committed by five desperadoes of Mexican descent, all of whom, from the vague reports available at the time, seemed to have been named Joaquín. A former Texas Ranger named Harry Love formed a posse of five men, each of whom was to be paid $150 for three months' work tracking down the five Joaquíns. After some weeks, Love and his men stumbled across a band of probable outlaws in the Tulare Valley, and killed the leader and at least one of his men. They sent the head of the supposed chief, pickled in a whiskey bottle, to the governor, demanding the reward of $1,000 being offered for the head of one of the Joaquíns. The idea that this was the head of the shadowy Joaquín Murieta gained currency, and the posse got the reward plus a substantial bonus. The famous head was exhibited around California's towns and mining camps, along with the presumed hand of Murieta's supposed right-hand man, Three-Fingered Jack. Whose head this really was, and whether there really was an outlaw named Joaquín Murieta, are questions to which history has supplied no answers. Californians in the 1850s generally believed that Joaquín Murieta was real, even though some, like the prominent but staid newspaper *Alta California*, proclaimed the pickled head a fraud. What *is* known is that a half-Cherokee Indian named John Rollin Ridge (known as Yellow Bird to his tribesmen) wrote and published in San Francisco in 1854 a small book entitled *The Life and Times of Joaquín Murieta*. This totally fictitious narrative created the Robin Hood legend of Joaquín Murieta that lived on for decades, to be revived by Hollywood long after the last survivor of the 1849 Gold Rush had departed the scene of these heroic adventures.

WILL BE EXHIBITED FOR ONE DAY ONLY! AT THE STOCKTON HOUSE! THIS DAY, AUG. 12, FROM 9 A. M., UNTIL 6, P. M. THE HEAD Of the renowned Bandit! JOAQUIN! AND THE HAND OF THREE FINGERED JACK! THE NOTORIOUS ROBBER AND MURDERER.

"JOAQUIN" and "THREE-FINGERED JACK," were captured by the State Rangers, under the command of Capt. Harry Love, at the Arroyo Cantina, July 24th. No reasonable doubt can be entertained in regard to the identification of the head now on exhibition, as being that of the notorious robber, Joaquin Murietta, as it has been recognised by hundreds of persons who have formerly seen him.

OPPOSITE: An ore wagon carrying silver- or gold-bearing ore from a Western mine to a mill where the valuable metal would be extracted from the rock. Once placer deposits were exhausted, throughout the West the emphasis shifted to what became known as hard-rock mining. Using picks and shovels, later adding drills and explosives, miners would chip pieces of metal-bearing ore from massive underground veins of quartz or other rock. The ore would be hoisted to the surface and then transported in wagons such as this to a stamping mill. Often one mill would serve a large mining district, so the distances these wagons covered could be substantial. In active areas long convoys of ore wagons would keep the stamping mills continually supplied. In the mills the ore would be crushed to a fine powder and combined with water and quicksilver (mercury in its liquid form). The quicksilver combined with the precious metal to form an amalgam, leaving the worthless rock to be discarded. The amalgam was then heated; this drew off the quicksilver, to be used again, leaving pure gold or silver to be molded into bars for shipment. (*Harper's Weekly*, September 14, 1878; I. P. Pranishnikoff, from a sketch by Henry R. Poore.)

ABOVE: A prospector leading a pack horse and riding with an Indian across a lonely stretch of Western terrain. Remington gave this sketch the title "Questionable Companionship." After the emphasis in Western mining shifted to hard-rock mining, there was still a role to be played by the lone prospector. Even in areas where there were no surface deposits to be panned, prospectors scoured the West looking for signs of a valuable strike. Not having the capital to set up mines themselves, prospectors later in the century sought to make their fortunes by finding potentially valuable claims and then selling them, often for modest sums, to be exploited by others. Stories of money made and opportunities missed circulated through the West like wildfire after the 1850s. A drifter named Bob Womack searched for years to find gold near Colorado's Cripple Creek; he eventually found it, but sold his claim when drunk for $300. Womack died in poverty years later after Cripple Creek had yielded millions to others. George Jackson discovered gold on Clear Creek, west of Denver, early in 1859. He sold this claim for a modest sum, then watched the Pike's Peak Gold Rush engulf the area. Jackson made another strike later at Ouray, Colorado, and sold that one for a more substantial $40,000. In Leadville, Colorado, a storekeeper named H. A. W. Tabor gave a $17 grubstake to two desperate prospectors, and a year later sold his share in their mine for $1 million. And so it went. Nothing died harder in the old West than the dream that there was a fortune to be made in the rocks just over the next hill. (*Harper's Weekly*, August 9, 1890; Frederic Remington.)

LEFT: Easterners viewed the life of Western mining camps and towns through a haze of sentimentality that originated in the writings of Bret Harte and others. As the century was drawing to a close, *Frank Leslie's* published this sketch of a miner at a lonely camp striken by bad news contained in a rare letter from home. (*Frank Leslie's Illustrated Newspaper*, May 31, 1890; Miss G. A. Davis.) BELOW: Dinner hour in a Western mining town in the 1880s. Despite the splendid names—every little boom town had its Grand Hotel and Delmonico's—the food and accommodations were liable to be on the primitive side. However, they were sumptuous compared to what had been available in the California mining camps of the 1850s. (*Harper's Weekly*, December 15, 1888; W. A. Rogers, from a sketch by Alfred Mitchell.) OPPOSITE: The lure of a potentially valuable strike often led prospectors onto Indian land. In remote areas they knew they might never be detected, and it was also often difficult, even impossible, to tell where the boundaries were. This group is searching the horizon for the U.S. troops who had driven them off a Cherokee reservation in 1890. The Cavalry could not always be stirred to maintain the integrity of Indian lands when violated by roving bands of prospectors. (*Frank Leslie's Illustrated Newspaper*, March 22, 1890; A. C. Redwood.)

BELOW: A Pike's Peaker, sketched by famed Western artist Albert Bierstadt, on the trail to the mining regions around Denver in the summer of 1859. The exact moment when gold was discovered in the Pike's Peak region is not recorded. There were reports of gold discoveries in 1858 that were intensified by news of George Jackson's definite strike early in 1859 on Clear Creek, 30 miles west of Denver. News of Jackson's discovery may be said to have started the Pike's Peak Gold Rush, the first attempt to exploit gold in the interior of the American West. Between 50,000 and 100,000 Easterners headed for Pike's Peak in the spring and summer of 1859. A few found gold, but many were unprepared for the hardships they would face and returned to the East disappointed.

After a slow start, mining in the Rockies expanded immensely when silver was found in huge quantities in the 1870s. (*Harper's Weekly*, August 13, 1859; Albert Bierstadt.) BOTTOM: A struggling group of Pike's Peakers making their way back East, having failed to strike it rich quickly in the diggings around Denver in the spring of 1859. The *Harper's* correspondent accompanying a military expedition reported passing thousands of dejected prospectors for whom Pike's Peak had been a bust. Compared to the numbers that went, so few were rewarded that for a time it was widely believed that Pike's Peak had been a hoax. It wasn't; there was gold in those hills, but it was difficult to reach, difficult to mine, food was scarce, supplies were expensive and the weather was much harsher than in the Sierra foothills of California. Those who arrived with no money on which to live, no tools or supplies and no knowledge of mining generally found themselves headed back East. Deaths from exhaustion and starvation on the return trail were commonplace. (*Harper's Weekly*, August 13, 1859; Albert Bierstadt.) OPPOSITE, TOP: Denver City in the summer of 1859 after the Pike's Peak Gold Rush was under way. Over the next 60 years perhaps $100 million worth of gold was extracted from the Pike's Peak region. *Leslie's* cautioned its readers against going to Pike's Peak without considering carefully whether they were suited to the arduous life of the miner. It stressed that prospectors should bring their own tools, supplies and money on which to live. Otherwise, they faced working as common laborers at $1 to $3 per day, as long as there was work, and had to consider the following chilling note, published in August 1859: "In a short time, probably by the middle of October, this whole region will be snowed under and frozen up, so as to put a stop to the working of sluices if not to mining altogether. There, then, for a period of at least six months, will be neither employment, food nor shelter within five hundred miles, and for those who are without provisions or money, there is literally nothing left but starvation." (*Frank Leslie's Illustrated Newspaper*, August 20, 1859.)

BELOW: A street in Gregory's Gulch, a mining town in the Pike's Peak region in 1860. The strikes around Gregory's Gulch were impressive enough for the town to see the establishment of its own quartz-stamping mill for processing ore from surrounding mines. (*Frank Leslie's Illustrated Newspaper*, December 15, 1860; Col. D. H. Huyett.)

OPPOSITE: An encounter with a grizzly bear in the Rocky Mountains—one of the hazards of the prospector's life. (*Frank Leslie's Illustrated Newspaper*, February 13, 1886; Paul Frenzeny.) BELOW: Prospectors in a Rocky Mountain hotel dining room, looking over an ore sample brought down from the surrounding hills by a hopeful prospector. By 1870 Colorado had replaced California as the nation's leading gold-producing state, and silver mining was growing into an even bigger Rocky Mountain industry. Silver mining differed from gold mining in many ways. Silver doesn't occur in the kind of placer deposits that first attracted prospectors to many of the gold-mining regions, but is almost always combined with quartz or some other mineral. Unlike gold, which is generally recognizable, silver in combination with other minerals can appear in many different colors, and can be difficult to detect. Definitive tests require the use of nitric and hydrochloric acid, which are dangerous to carry into the field. The traditional procedure was for the prospector to bring an ore sample back to town where it could be tested, keeping the location of his new claim to himself. Tests would reveal how rich the ore sample was. If it seemed likely to be worthwhile, the prospector would do some work on the claim, and record it if he could, to establish his ownership. Then would come the search, usually disappointing, for a buyer with the capital to develop the claim, build the mines and supply everything else needed to make money from hard-rock mining. Fraud was not unknown—salting worthless claims with rich pieces of ore in order to make a quick sale to a novice buyer—nor was the expropriation of claims by force or deception. It sometimes seemed to Easterners that everyone from the mayor to the hotel porters in a Rocky Mountain town owned a claim somewhere in the surrounding hills and had an ore sample to show you on demand. The vast majority never panned out, but, as seen here, a new sample was always the subject of lively curiosity. (*Harper's Weekly*, August 30, 1887; A. C. Redwood, from a sketch by Alfred Mitchell.) OVERLEAF: A group of Rocky Mountain prospectors on their way to a new location. For a difficult trip through largely uncharted hills, with all possessions loaded onto wagons pulled by mule teams, it made sense to join together for protection. Once the new diggings were reached, it would be every man for himself in the search for the best claims. (*Harper's Weekly*, May 1, 1875; Frenzeny and Tavernier.)

OPPOSITE: An avalanche in the Rocky Mountains catches three prospectors in the mountains above Leadville by surprise. (*Harper's Weekly*, September 1, 1888; Barnard and Graham.) ABOVE: Not all mining in the West was for precious metals. The Colorado Coal and Iron Company had a large coal mine at Crested Butte where in 1884 an explosion of unknown origin set fire to the lower levels of the mine, killing about 60 miners by suffocation and burning. In this view the recovered bodies of the victims have been laid out in a shed. The inset picture shows victims being carried out of the mine. (*Harper's Weekly*, February 16, 1884; from photographs by George E. Mellen.)

ABOVE: A lively trial scene in a Colorado mining town in 1886. New towns in the mining regions were ephemeral until it was clear that there was enough valuable ore in the vicinity to build the trappings of a permanent settlement—courthouses, etc. Until that time, municipal business was typically conducted in the local saloon, often with the saloon keeper presiding. In the face of this company, one may assume that most lawyers were willing to heed the warning posted on the wall. (*Frank Leslie's Illustrated Newspaper*, November 27, 1886; Alfred Mitchell.) OPPOSITE: Magnificent Colorado scenery forms the backdrop to another column of miners on their way to a new strike, this time across a mountain on a road of logs. After the 1859 Rush to the Pike's Peak region, the population of the area around Denver grew so fast that the Colorado Territory was soon administratively separated from Kansas. In 1876 Colorado became a state as one valuable strike after another, both gold and silver, guaranteed the permanent importance of this new mining area. In time a network of narrow-gauge railroad lines would fan out from Denver and make access to many of Colorado's remote areas easier than by the route depicted here. (*Frank Leslie's Illustrated Newspaper*, May 24, 1879.)

OVERLEAF: A panoramic view of the Rocky Mountain mining town of Leadville, Colorado, based on a photograph taken in 1888 by the company of one of the pioneer Western photographers, William Henry Jackson of Denver. Leadville, almost two miles above sea level, had a history that is a microcosm of the pattern of Western mining in the last decades of the century. Gold was found on the site of the later city of Leadville in 1860. For a couple of years prospectors braved the elements and the altitude to work these placer deposits, which were soon played out. Then for about ten years, from 1863 to 1873, the area was abandoned. In the mid-1870s the prospectors returned and a new discovery was made, not of gold, but of rich silver ore in the form of carbonate of lead, from which the silver-mining town took its name. The silver ore was so rich that by the end of 1879, Leadville had a population of 15,000 and was yielding over $12 million worth of silver annually. Before the silver deposits were exhausted toward the end of the century, Leadville had produced about $200 million. Later still, copper and zinc mining helped maintain the area's prosperity. (*Harper's Weekly*, December 1, 1888; from a photograph by W. H. Jackson & Co.)

ABOVE: The main street of Virginia City in the mid-1870s, the peak years of mining on Nevada's legendary Comstock Lode. During this period, the many rich mines of the Comstock, in the area dominated by Mt. Davidson in the Washoe Range, were yielding approximately $36 million in silver annually. So much silver was coming out of the Comstock that a branch of the U.S. Mint was established nearby at Carson City. Within 25 years after this view was drawn, and after one of the gaudiest chapters in the history of Western mining, Virginia City and its twin boom town of Gold Hill, a mile away, would be largely deserted. The Carson City Mint would be closed and the mines of the fabulous Comstock would be either played out or flooded. The exact moment when precious metals were first found in the Washoe area is not known. The first prospectors in the area, interested only in gold, discarded the rich silver ore that would later make most of Washoe's fortune. Excitement followed discoveries in 1859, when the town of Gold Hill was founded. Later that year the discovery of what would become the famous Ophir Mine, named after the source of King Solomon's fortune, created the second Washoe boom town of Virginia City. The "worthless" silver had by then been identified, and the following year saw a rush of thousands of miners across the Sierra from California. Whoever was the first to realize the full potential of the Washoe area, it was almost certainly not a shadowy character named Henry Thomas Paige Comstock. Quite possibly without any legitimate claim, and simply by the force of his choleric personality, Comstock seems to have muscled in on the Ophir in time to share the first profits. In the tradition of Western prospecting, Comstock and his associates sold the Ophir early for less than $100,000 and moved on, Comstock to an impoverished and alcoholic suicide a decade later in Bozeman, Montana. However, he left his name attached to the huge, fragmented body of fabulously rich ore that lay beneath the surface of Washoe. Exploitation of the Comstock Lode continued for decades after Comstock himself was only a dim memory to the region's earliest pioneers. Before it was over, it produced almost $400 million in silver and gold. Among those who profited was a young entrepreneur named George Hearst, who parlayed a modest investment into the foundation of one of the country's great newspaper fortunes. Even by the rich standards of Western boom towns, Virginia City in its heyday was something special. Reaching a peak population of about 25,000 in the 1870s, it boasted more than its share of elaborate mansions, owned mostly by the San Francisco financiers who controlled the mines, restaurants, hotels, saloons, whorehouses and gambling dens. The ubiquitous Edwin Booth played Hamlet to large crowds at Piper's Opera House, where Joseph Jefferson also appeared and where Maude Adams made her debut in 1877. A decade earlier humorist Artemus Ward had had a hugely successful run at Maguire's New Opera House, and the notorious Adah Isaacs Menken became one of Virginia City's favorite attractions in the melodrama *Mazeppa*, based on Byron's poem, in which she appeared in flesh-colored tights tied to a trained horse. It was in the columns of Virginia City's newspaper *The Territorial Enterprise* that in 1863 a young journalist from Missouri first signed an article with the pseudonym Mark Twain. The following year an incident described either as a quarrel with a fellow newspaperman or as an outrageous practical joke forced Twain to leave the area hurriedly. He went to California, while his Nevada reminiscences, *Roughing It*, later became one of the classics of Western literature. (*Frank Leslie's Illustrated Newspaper*, March 2, 1878.) OPPOSITE: An unusual form of Western entertainment, two daredevil lumberjacks "shooting a flume" in the Sierra Nevada. There was no timber in the immediate area of the Comstock Lode's mines and towns. By the middle of the 1870s the mines alone required 80 million board feet of lumber a year for shoring up tunnels and mine shafts, and about 250,000 cords of firewood annually to power steam engines. The V-shaped flume was invented to carry lumber from the Sierra to the floor of the Washoe Valley. It was then hauled up to the mines of the Comstock on the narrow-gauge Virginia and Truckee Railroad. Before the Comstock was played out, a stretch of Sierra forest at least 100 miles long had been stripped for wood to supply it. (*Harper's Weekly*, June 2, 1877; Graham and Day.)

The changing of a shift at a Comstock Lode silver mine in the mid-1870s. The miners are checking in at the controller's office before descending the mine shafts in the elevators in the background. The Comstock was so rich that by the mid-1860s the area had a full-fledged miners' union that won for its members many gains that placed them ahead of their laboring counterparts elsewhere in the United States. Chief among these were the eight-hour day and the unusual pay scale of $4 a day, regardless of experience, considerably more than laborers could expect to earn in the industrial East. "Think of a city," Mark Twain wrote, "with not one solitary poor man in it." Despite these gains, the life of a Comstock Lode silver miner was not totally enviable. Accidents were common, and doctors were few. The water in the area was bad and caused many deaths in the early years. Nothing was known about lung diseases caused by rock dust. Subterranean fires, cave-ins, falls down mine shafts and explosions were daily possibilities, as miners struggled to free the ore hundreds of feet below the earth's surface in temperatures that often surpassed 120 degrees Fahrenheit. Perhaps 300 miners were killed in accidents in 30 years on the Comstock, a low figure considering the numbers involved. (*Harper's Weekly*, August 25, 1877; Paul Frenzeny.)

RIGHT: Miners descending a shaft of the huge Consolidated Virginia Mine in Virginia City. The elevators were covered with metal roofs to protect miners from falling rocks. As the elevators descended 1,550 feet in 40 seconds, the only illumination came from the candle-powered lanterns that the miners carried. *Frank Leslie's* reported that about 5,000 candles were consumed every day in the Consolidated Virginia Mine. (*Frank Leslie's Illustrated Newspaper*, March 9, 1878.) BELOW: Miners at a landing 1,550 feet beneath the surface in the Consolidated Virginia Mine. By 1865 the Comstock's first major strikes were played out at the 500-foot level and above, but deeper ore bodies were soon discovered. The Consolidated Virginia Mine and its neighbor, the California Mine, were the major beneficiaries of the great silver strike in October 1873 known to Western mining history as the Big Bonanza. The Big Bonanza, at the 1,167-foot level, more than justified its name. Its richest ore proved to be worth between $1,000 and $10,000 a ton, and in the ensuing years brought a gross yield to the owners of the Consolidated Virginia of $150 million, of which about 40% was profit. In 1877, the year the *Frank Leslie's* artists visited the mines and created this unique pictorial record of hard-rock mining in the West, the Comstock reached its peak yield of about $36 million in gold and silver. By the end of the 1870s a general decline had begun. The 1880s saw a brief revival, partly the result of new technologies that allowed old claims to be reworked with profit. Soon after 1890 the final decline set in, and by the end of the century the story of the Comstock was over. (*Frank Leslie's Illustrated Newspaper*, March 9, 1878.)

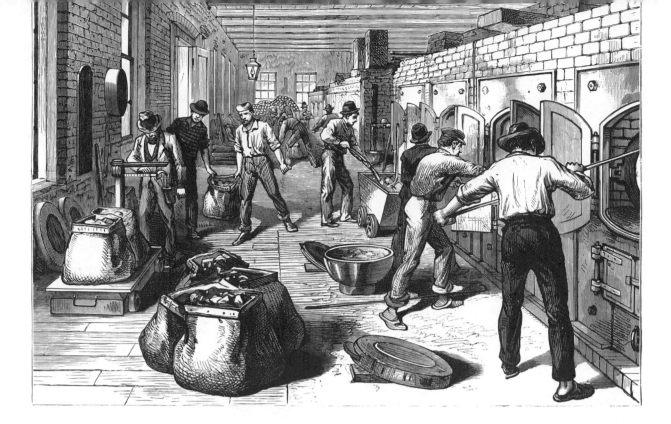

OPPOSITE: A miner wielding his pick in the Consolidated Virginia Mine. Miners wore the minimum of clothes because of the heat. Usually they were only assigned for a week at a time to the hottest areas underground. Hundreds of feet below the surface, the enemy of the hard-rock miner was water. The Consolidated Virginia had the best equipment then available to drain water from its lower tunnels. Many Western mines were closed when the cost of continually draining them surpassed the profits that could reasonably be expected. On the Comstock, which always did things on a larger scale than elsewhere, an attempt was made to solve the drainage problem permanently by a California engineer named Adolf Sutro. He proposed building a huge tunnel through the whole mining area. The tunnel eventually worked fairly well, but the cost was vast. By the time it was finished in 1878, after 15 years of legal and financial wrangling, the greatest days of the Comstock were already in the past. (*Frank Leslie's Illustrated Newspaper*, March 9, 1878; T. de Thulstrup.) ABOVE: Workmen in a Virginia City retort house. They are removing quicksilver, to be used again, from the silver amalgam created earlier in the refining process. The dried amalgam was brought to the retort house in the large canvas bags seen in the foreground. When heated in the retorts on the right, the quicksilver was drained off, leaving pure silver to be cast into bars

in the assay office. (*Frank Leslie's Illustrated Newspaper*, April 20, 1878.) BELOW: Workmen in the assay office molding the melted bullion into bars. At times, the Comstock mills tried to prevent robbery by producing silver in bars so large that no one man could carry them. (*Frank Leslie's Illustrated Newspaper*, April 20, 1878.) OVERLEAF: This view from the 1877 *Frank Leslie's* expedition gives a good idea of the size of the ore-refining establishments that serviced the Comstock Lode. This is part of the equipment in which the crushed ore was combined with water to form a muddy "pulp." Quicksilver was then introduced to separate out the silver from the rock. Less than 30 years after the discovery of gold in California, the precious-metal industry in the West had developed to the point where these huge installations would be erected in any spot that promised a steady supply of rich ore. Mining technology advanced rapidly by trial and error after the Gold Rush. In the 1860s it cost $50 to process a ton of silver ore. A decade later, this cost had been reduced to $12. Concurrently, the amount of silver recovered increased from about 65% to 85% of the pure silver present. Later advances would increase this percentage still further. Mechanical drills powered by compressed air, dynamite for blasting and mine-ventilation systems were also improved by the experience of miners on the Comstock. (*Frank Leslie's Illustrated Newspaper*, April 13, 1878.)

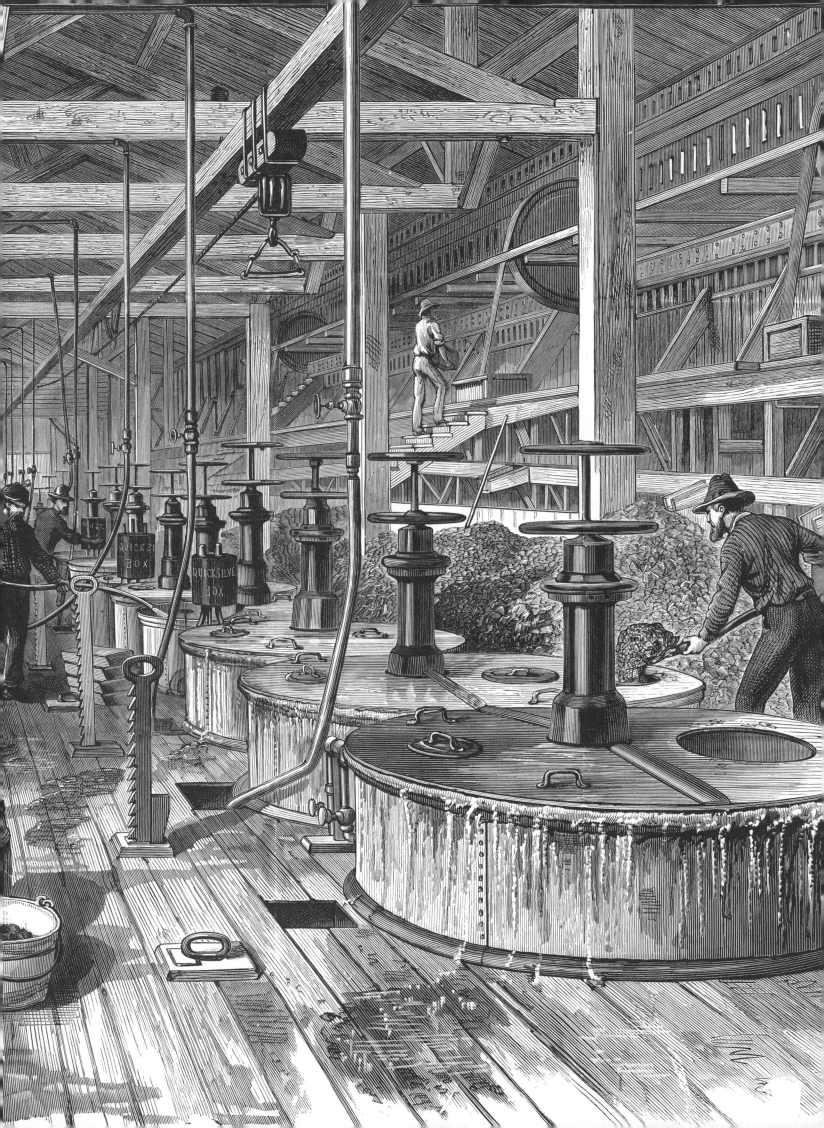

ABOVE: A hopeful prospector packing his horse to head for the Black Hills of South Dakota in 1876, two years after a military expedition under George Armstrong Custer had discovered gold in that region. By 1877 there were 7,000 prospectors in the Black Hills, where the town of Deadwood was the center of the mining area. Though the Sioux who owned the Black Hills by treaty refused offers from the federal government to buy it back, they were eventually simply forced off the land to clear the way for its commercial exploitation. (*Harper's Weekly*, October 14, 1876; I. P. Pranishnikoff.) OPPOSITE, TOP: Labor unrest mixed with racial violence in September 1885 at the Rock Springs, Wyoming, coal mines run by the Union Pacific Railroad to provide fuel for their trains. For some years the railroad had employed only white miners at Rock Springs at salaries of $8 to $10 per day. When the miners struck for higher wages, the railroad turned the mines over to contractors who hit on the idea of bringing in several hundred Chinese laborers who would accept lower wages. A mob of white miners launched a violent attack that resulted in 28 deaths among the Chinese contingent. This was one of the worst outbreaks of violence between white and Chinese miners in the West. Federal troops were brought in to protect the Chinese workers, and many of their attackers were arrested. (*Harper's Weekly*, September 26, 1885; T. de Thulstrup, from photographs by Lt. C. A. Booth.)

RIGHT: The arrival of the first woman to reach a gold-mining camp in the Coeur d'Alene area of northern Idaho in 1884. The Coeur d'Alene did not prove to be the site of one of the bigger Western mineral strikes, but the romantic, isolated life of the Western mining camp provided an enduring myth for the sentimental Eastern press. As the frontier closed toward the end of the century, the mining areas that were still productive settled into the unromantic, difficult, day-to-day business of yielding worthwhile amounts of ore. The Western prospector's last gasp sent thousands to the Klondike River after gold was discovered there in 1896, but the terrain and climate were difficult and few struck it rich. The exercise did give the population of Alaska a permanent boost. (*Frank Leslie's Illustrated Newspaper*, April 19, 1884.)

Settling the West

THE AMERICAN FRONTIER moved West in slow and tentative stages after the American Revolution. Lewis and Clark reached the Pacific in the first decade of the new century. In Oregon they found a rich, fertile land that had only been explored by a few fur trappers, traders, mountain men and missionaries. At that time, however, even the Ohio River was still far beyond the western horizon of the original 13 states located along the Atlantic coastline of North America, and there was little interest in setting out across an uncharted wilderness for the Pacific Northwest.

This situation changed as the nineteenth century got under way. The Louisiana Purchase added an immense new area to the nation's territory, and served in part to turn attention toward the interior of the continent. Gradually the uncharted wilderness beyond the Mississippi was further explored and mapped. Robert Stuart, a fur trader, traveled over much of what became known as the Oregon Trail in 1812–13, at which time he made the crucial discovery of the South Pass through the Rockies. South Pass, in present Wyoming, made the Oregon Trail possible. It was the only place north of New Mexico where wagons could cross the mountains.

The first settlers from the eastern United States to reach Oregon arrived in the Willamette Valley in 1832, after traveling the Oregon Trail guided by one of the legendary mountain men, William Sublette. In 1836 a small party led by a Protestant missionary, Dr. Marcus Whitman, left Leavenworth, Kansas, for Oregon with two wagons. Though they had to abandon their wagons along the way, the Whitman party continued on foot and reached Oregon. This was a memorable event because the group included the first two white women, so far as anyone knows, to cross the Continental Divide. One of them, Whitman's wife, Narcissa, kept a valuable diary of her experiences on the trail. This story doesn't have a happy ending; Whitman and his wife were both killed by the Cayuse Indians a few years later.

By 1840 the route West was well known. The first real wagon train on the Oregon Trail left Sapling, Missouri, on May 19, 1841, with 69 pioneers, including five women, seven children and 12 wagons. They were guided by a veteran mountain man named Tom Fitzpatrick. This group, known after its leaders as the Bidwell–Bartleson Party, split into two groups west of South Pass. One group went to Oregon; the other group became the first party of emigrants to reach California overland. Neither group reached its destination with wagons intact.

In 1843 a much larger wagon train, accompanied by the enterprising Dr. Whitman, finally reached Oregon with wagons still rolling. The following year the first wagons were brought across the Sierra, at Truckee Pass, to California. Two hundred settlers came West on the Oregon/California Trail in 1842, 1,000 in 1843, 5,000 in 1845. With the discovery of gold in California in 1848, travel on the Trail exploded. More than 30,000 came West in 1849 and 55,000 more in 1850, the peak year. By 1857, 165,000 had crossed the continent overland. By 1869, when the first transcontinental railroad was completed, 350,000 emigrants had journeyed West on the Oregon/California Trail. The railroads gradually took over, but wagon trains continued to roll out of Missouri every May for 20 years after 1869; it was cheaper than taking a large family by train, and remained the only way for a farmer with livestock to move West.

The Oregon/California Trail began in western Missouri at Independence and the other Missouri River towns. It followed the North Fork of the Platte River across present-day Kansas and Nebraska, and then the Sweetwater River to South Pass, where the Continental Divide was crossed. West of South Pass, the trails for Oregon and California diverged. The route to Oregon curved past Soda Springs and Fort Hall and followed the Snake River north to the Blue Mountains. The final leg, down the Columbia River to the Willamette Valley, was often traveled on rafts.

Routes to California cut off from the Oregon Trail at several places west of South Pass including Fort Bridger, Soda Springs and Fort Hall. It was possible to reach California by routes either north or south of Great Salt Lake. Most chose the former route, and all routes came together to follow the Humboldt River until it disappeared in the desert in present-day Nevada. A murderous desert crossing then brought the settlers to the passes through the Sierra Nevada Mountains to California.

Not all those who packed up their children and livestock, and headed West on the Oregon/California Trail, went all the way to the Pacific. The Homestead Act of 1862, pushed through Congress by free-soil advocates during the Civil War, provided that anyone could claim 160 acres of public land in the West by living on it and farming it for five continuous years. In the first six months after the Act was passed, over 200,000 acres in Kansas and Nebraska were claimed by hopeful farmers. The Homestead Act lured many to try their hands at farming in other areas as well.

Even though the land was free, making a go of it as a farmer proved to be more difficult than many expected. A great deal of the most fertile farmland was already in private hands when the Homestead Act was passed, and many followed the lure of free land to remote areas that were not ideal for growing anything. In some areas, 160 acres was simply not enough with which to create a viable agricultural enterprise. Some took up the government's offer without any knowledge of farming. Others had knowledge but little or no capital with which to see even a modest farm started. Many failed to meet the five-year requirement when economic necessity forced them off their land to seek work elsewhere. In 1890, almost 30 years after the passage of the Homestead Act, it was calculated that no more than one homesteader in three had been successful enough to obtain final title to his land.

Whatever the problems they might eventually encounter, the dream of independence certainly brought tens of thousands across the Mississippi in the decades after the Civil War. When the transcontinental railroad was completed in 1869, the pace of farmers moving West to take advantage of the Homestead Act increased dramatically. Kansas and Nebraska, though within the reach of many even before the railroad had been built, had a combined population of less than half a million in 1870. By 1890 each state had over a million citizens. In 1870 Oregon and Washington had fewer than 100,000 settlers. Twenty years later their combined population was almost 700,000. Even out-of-the-way Arizona, in the same time span, saw its non-Indian population increase from 10,000 to 90,000. Where people went to settle, civilization gradually followed. Stagecoach and telegraph lines linked previously inaccessible areas with the East and with each other. More and more railroads came, towns and even cities were established. Rough frontier justice, often arbitrary and unfair, was gradually supplanted by courts and duly constituted authorities. By the end of the nineteenth century the process of settling had changed the face of the West completely.

OPPOSITE: Settlers escaping from the flooding Missouri River at Vermillion, Dakota Territory, in the spring of 1881. (*Frank Leslie's Illustrated Newspaper*, April 16, 1881.)

OPPOSITE, TOP: The Broadway in St. Louis, Missouri, in the 1850s. St. Louis, St. Joseph and particularly Independence, Missouri, were the major starting points for overland travel to the West. Bustling street scenes such as this would have been encountered in the spring of any year in these famous river towns as wagon trains were fitted out and supplies secured for the long overland journey to Oregon or California. Established as a trading post by the French in 1764, St. Louis quickly became one of the hubs of Western travel. In 1806 the whole town turned out to welcome Lewis and Clark home from their 7,000-mile journey to the Pacific. Later in the century, St. Joseph gained fame as the Eastern terminus of the Pony Express and the starting point of the freight-carrying wagon trains of Russell, Majors & Waddell. Heavy-freight hauling, particularly to the mining regions of the West, represented the major business of the firm, which also sponsored the short-lived Pony Express. By the early 1830s Independence had become the starting point of the Oregon Trail, the major road West through the Missouri, Platte and Snake River valleys to the Pacific Northwest. In the Oregon Trail's peak years in the 1840s and 1850s, thousands of emigrants came through Independence each spring. (*The Illustrated London News*, May 1, 1858.) OPPOSITE, BOTTOM: A family on one of the overland trails, heading from Arkansas to Texas in the 1870s. Even after the first transcontinental railroad had been completed, this mode of travel remained common in less settled areas. (*Harper's Weekly*,

April 4, 1874; Frenzeny and Tavernier.) ABOVE: The Oregon/California Trail had been in full operation for 30 years, and was in the process of being supplanted by the railroad, when *Harper's* published this lurid little drawing of Indians on the plains gambling for possession of the attractive female captive seen tied to a wagon wheel in the background. Though there were certainly some violent incidents, the danger of Indian attack on the Oregon/California Trail was actually not great. Across the plains, the route passed through a sort of no-man's-land—in which few Indians were likely to be encountered—between the Pawnee to the north and the Cheyenne to the south. A deterrent to violence when Indians did appear was the fact that the largest wagon trains obviously had more firepower than any small party of raiding Indians. At peak season in the Trail's most active years, there might also be several wagon trains within sight of each other at many times, so the pioneers were hardly alone in the wilderness. Indians met with on the plains would more likely want to trade some buffalo meat for tobacco than engage in a battle they were likely to lose. The Indian danger on the Trail meant mostly that animals would be stolen if they got loose and ran off, and solitary hunters might be in danger if they rode away from the wagon trains to look for game, particularly if they rode desirable horses. Documented accounts of all-out assaults on wagon trains are rare; for the pioneer, cholera was a much more formidable foe. (*Harper's Weekly*, March 26, 1870; W. M. Cary.)

RIGHT: A scene from the end of the California Trail: a small winter encampment in the Sierra Nevada Mountains. This view was reprinted in *The Illustrated London News* from Frémont's *Report of the Exploring Expeditions of 1842 and 1843–44*. The *Report*, published in 1845, was required reading thereafter among more literate emigrants, but many failed to grasp one of its important messages: Frémont and his men were experienced explorers, capable of surviving indefinitely under wilderness conditions with which the average emigrants, mostly farmers and their families, were totally unprepared to cope. Nowhere are the hazards of the last part of the journey to California clearer than in the story of the ill-fated Donner party. George Donner, an affluent Illinois farmer, and his wagon train left Independence in the spring of 1846. In present-day Wyoming, the train split into two groups. One group pressed on to California via the Fort Hall route without incident. Donner and 88 others, however, decided to try a new route that they had read about in Lansford W. Hastings' *Emigrant's Guide to Oregon and California*. Hastings recommended a cutoff from the Fort Hall route running south of Salt Lake and then straight west across the Great Salt Lake Desert. The book stressed the saving of mileage, which proved illusory, and minimized the difficulties of the arduous desert crossing. Traveling without an experienced guide, the Donner party found the going very slow west of Salt Lake, and crucial time slipped away before they found their way across the desert. It was late October when they reached the Sierra; the snows came before the mountains could be crossed. A scouting party was sent ahead to try to cross the mountains and find help, but it was already far too late. The weather closed in as Donner and his party prepared for the winter without enough food or adequate shelter. In the unforgiving Sierra Nevada winter, Donner saw his dream of a new life in California disintegrate into a nightmare of hunger, famine, insanity and cannibalism. When rescuers reached them in the spring, Donner and almost half of his party were dead. The survivors, barely alive and clinging to the remnants of their sanity, were led slowly over the mountains to California. It was some time before another party of emigrants could be persuaded to try Donner's route. (*The Illustrated London News*, January 10, 1846.)

BELOW: A mounted bugler summons the members of a Western-bound wagon train to prepare for the day's travel. The foothills of the Rocky Mountains loom in the background. After weeks crossing the prairies of Nebraska, this party is about to encounter the formidable hazards of the last part of the journey: mountains, deserts and difficult river crossings. One feature of life on the Oregon/California Trail that caused many to fail was that the most difficult physical work came at the end of the trip when men and animals were tired, supplies were thin and equipment was worn out. Note the slogan, "To the Diggings," on the second wagon from the left. By the time this picture was published in 1856, many hopeful prospectors had headed to the gold-mining regions by wagon train on the Oregon/California Trail, but the argonauts of the Gold Rush were, as a rule, young men who didn't travel with women and children. The picture therefore makes an important point; often wagon trains were formed by the chance combination of groups. Here, perhaps, a party of farmers and their families bound for Oregon has joined forces for mutual protection with a group of miners headed for the gold fields of California. (*Ballou's Pictorial Drawing-Room Companion*, 1856; John Andrew.)

Horses being driven into a corral formed by the wagons. This was done every night on the trail to keep the animals from running off or being stolen by Indians. Horses were not used to pull the wagons, but were ridden alongside. Those without horses usually walked to preserve the strength of the mules or oxen that did pull the wagons. Generally, six mules or oxen, in yokes of two each, were the minimum. Mules pulled the wagons faster, but oxen were cheaper. Oxen had the further advantage of not being coveted nearly as much as mules by Indians, and oxen could also feed on grass along the trail while mules had to be fed grain carried on board. Considering that oxen could also be eaten in an emergency, most emigrants, sometimes at their peril, discounted the two weeks that mules could save them and opted for the slower animals. Cows were sometimes trailed alongside to provide milk. The wagons, smaller, lighter versions of the Eastern Conestoga, cost about $60 to $90, and were not particularly maneuverable. Spare parts were carried along, especially axles and other parts needed to repair the wooden wheels and their iron tires. Food on the trail was simple—bacon, biscuits, coffee, dried fruit, molasses and whatever game could be killed or traded for with the Indians along the way. Note the soldier's cap worn by the man in the foreground. As the Gold Rush provided the first great spur to Western emigration, the end of the Civil War provided the second. Thousands of veterans went West in the later 1860s. Some of the wagons shown here are heavily laden with furniture and farming equipment. Many parties started the journey West with every imaginable possession, not excluding pianos and grandfather clocks. As wagons broke down, as animals tired or died and as the trail itself, once the Continental Divide had been crossed, became more treacherous, heaps of this material would be left behind. It is about 2,000 miles from Independence, Missouri, to Oregon's Columbia River. Scheduling was critical. If the wagon trains left Missouri too early in the spring, the grass on the plains wouldn't be high enough to feed the animals. If they left too late, they risked reaching the Sierra without enough time to cross before winter. Covering 12 to 15 miles a day, the pioneers found they had very little extra time to spend fording rivers, repairing wagons, resting and tending the sick. (*Harper's Weekly*, June 12, 1869; Theodore R. Davis.)

BELOW: A group of guides and wagon drivers settled around an evening campfire as a large wagon train pulls in behind them for the night. The day on the Oregon/California Trail began early. Women and children rode in the wagons while men walked alongside. A long rest was taken at noon to allow the animals to graze and conserve their energy in the heat of the summer day. One of the most difficult things the pioneers had to do was cross rivers and streams; this called for all the experience the guides and drivers could muster. Whether it was attempted by raft or by removing the wheels and floating the wagons across, disaster lurked everywhere, since the clumsy wagons simply weren't designed for it. Many people drowned and many wagons were lost in the attempt. (*Harper's Weekly*, December 23, 1871; A. R. Waud.)

OVERLEAF: A wagon train attacked by Indians. This view of pioneers defending their wagon during an Indian attack was published less than three months after Custer's debacle on the Little Big Horn. *Harper's*, interestingly, used the opportunity to unleash a scathing attack on the Indian policy of the federal government: "It is undeniable that all our Indian wars have been provoked by the whites. Every treaty made with the Indians has been violated as soon as it was for the interest of the whites to break it. Despoiled of their lands, demoralized by whiskey, taught treachery and fraud by the 'superior race', it is but natural that they should fight for the possession of their lands." (*Harper's Weekly*, September 16, 1876; first published in the [London] *Graphic*, August 26, 1876; John S. Davis.)

OPPOSITE, TOP: Two scenes in the life of a newly arrived family in the West: building their first home (a log cabin) and laying their fences—in both cases with the help of neighbors. (*Harper's Weekly,* January 24, 1874; Frenzeny and Tavernier.) OPPOSITE, BOTTOM: A Kansas farmer plowing his land for the first time. *Harper's* reported that many found the prairie so hard that three or four yoke of oxen were often needed to pull the plow the first time the land was broken. (*Harper's Weekly,* May 9, 1868; Theodore R. Davis.) ABOVE: Prairie fires were the great danger faced by pioneer farmers, particularly in the dry late-summer and early-autumn seasons. Here a homesteader, with the flames of a large fire looming across the prairie, is running a fireguard—plowing a wide strip of land that he hopes will stop the fire before it reaches his crops or cabin. In many areas it was common to plow fireguards right after harvest as the dry season approached, but fires often came up suddenly and found pioneer farmers unprepared. (*Harper's Weekly,* March 28, 1868; Theodore R. Davis.)

Three views illustrating hazards faced by settlers in the West. OPPOSITE, TOP: A family on the Missouri River near Fort Peck in northern Montana Territory. *Harper's* reported that after they had watched the river rise by as much as six feet within 24 hours, these settlers wisely sawed their cabin in half. The half nearer the river was washed downstream, leaving only a forlorn chimney where it stood, but the rest of their home was saved. (*Harper's Weekly*, September 18, 1875; W. M. Cary.) OPPOSITE, BOTTOM: A farmer and his wife in a Kansas windstorm. This view is occasionally reproduced to illustrate windstorms encountered by Western-bound wagon trains. Actually, this type of small covered wagon drawn by just two horses would only have served for local transportation; teams of oxen or mules pulled the wagon trains West. This farmer appears to be attempting to deliver a load of hay. (*Harper's Weekly*, May 30, 1874; Frenzeny and Tavernier.) ABOVE: After settlers had survived floods in the spring and fires in the summer, winter brought its own perils. This view shows the dramatic rescue of a California family whose cabin had been buried for two days and nights under 15 feet of snow by a Sierra Nevada avalanche in Woodford's Canyon. (*Frank Leslie's Illustrated Newspaper*, March 29, 1884; Lagarde Measom.) OVERLEAF: Away from the prairie in more wooded areas, forest fires were a perennial hazard. This view records the burning of the little town of Peshtigo, Wisconsin, on the Northern frontier in 1871. Over a million acres of timber burned in this fire following the same hot, dry summer that had preceded the great Chicago fire a few hundred miles to the south. (*Harper's Weekly*, November 25, 1871.)

ABOVE: As seen in this 1890 illustration, the covered wagon was still very much in use as the frontier era in American history was drawing to its close. On February 2, 1890, 11 million acres of former Sioux reservation land in South Dakota were made available for sale to homesteaders at nominal prices. The payments were to go to the Indians, who had been moved to a smaller reservation. The opening of this territory did not bring a rush comparable to the opening of the Oklahoma Territory a year earlier. This was a hard, cold land, difficult to reach and difficult to farm. (*Harper's Weekly*, March 8, 1890; Charles Graham.) OPPOSITE, TOP: As the farming frontier gathered momentum, it did not take long for agriculture on a huge scale to reach areas that had been empty prairie a few years earlier. This view of steam-powered wheat-threshing equipment on the huge Dalrymple farm west of Fargo in the Dakota Territory was drawn in 1878, less than a decade after the first wheat crop was grown in the Red River Valley. Dalrymple employed 400 men, 500 horses, 80 mechanical reapers and a great deal of other modern equipment. This type of farming was very profitable in an era of plentiful land and cheap labor and transportation costs. *Frank Leslie's* correspondent, accustomed to the smaller scale of Eastern farming, was astonished at a farm so big that managers of different sections communicated with each other by telegraph. This view was based in part on photographs by F. Jay Haynes, one of the legendary pioneer photographers. (*Frank Leslie's Illustrated Newspaper*, October 19, 1878; Albert Berghaus, based on sketches by George H. Ellsbury and photographs by F. Jay Haynes.) OPPOSITE, BOTTOM: A party of farm laborers on their way to a wheat farm along the line of the Northern Pacific Railroad in the Dakotas in 1890. (*Harper's Weekly*, December 13, 1890; W. A. Rogers.)

ABOVE: Where homesteaders moved West to settle, towns sprang up, their location often determined by proximity to the means of transportation, whether river or railroad. As with Western railroads, mines and farms, some towns survived and some did not. Here, ravenous wolves patrol the empty, ruined streets of a busted town in Kansas in the 1870s, while in the background the railroad passes through another part of the country. This scene was repeated countless times when little prairie villages were bypassed by railroad builders. While this may have been a composite portrait of many such towns, Robert Taft offers some reasons why it may be a view of the deserted town of Zarah in Kansas' Benton County. Zarah was a bustling little town in 1872 that quickly died when the Santa Fe Railroad bypassed it by only about a mile. (*Harper's Weekly*, February 28, 1874; Frenzeny and Tavernier.) OPPOSITE, TOP: A bustling market-day scene in Parsons City, Kansas, in 1873, a year and a half after the town was founded. Opened to settlement by the Kansas–Nebraska Act of 1854, Kansas was the scene of violent conflict between pro- and antislavery forces in the years before the Civil War. After entering the Union as a free state in 1861, Kansas witnessed the whole panorama of Western history in the next 20 years. By the late 1870s the great buffalo herds were wiped out, the first railroads were built and the remaining hostile Indians were subdued. The railroads brought prosperity to a succession of Kansas cattle towns, including Wichita, Dodge City, Ellsworth and Abilene, to which Texas cattlemen drove their herds for shipment East. The era of the great cattle drives ended by the mid-1880s, however, when the railroads themselves reached Texas, and Kansas settled into a long period when her economy would be dominated by agriculture. Everywhere on the farming frontier, sleepy little towns like this one came alive once a week on market day when farmers and their families came to sell their produce and to buy whatever supplies they needed. (*Harper's Weekly*, November 8, 1873; Frenzeny and Tavernier.) OPPOSITE, BOTTOM: On the treeless prairie, lumber for building was at a premium in the early years, and some little towns were at first essentially comprised of dugouts with roofs. The sign "Hides Bought" suggests Kansas in the buffalo-hunting era of the early 1870s. With the railroad tracks running right through the center of this little village, it could probably look forward to a more prosperous future. (*Harper's Weekly*, April 4, 1874; Frenzeny and Tavernier.)

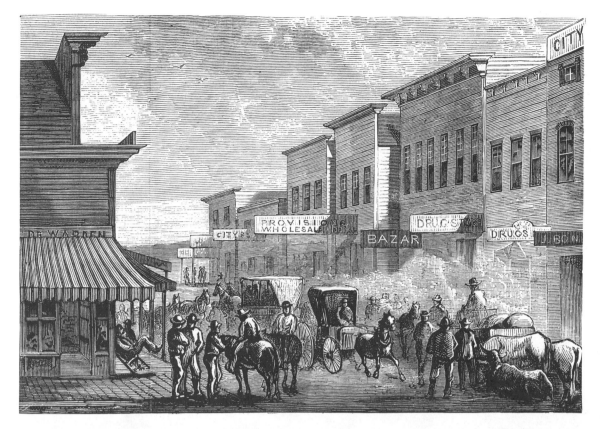

IZENY & TAVERNIER

ABOVE: Dogs and pigs share the street with horses and cattle in Atchison, Kansas, just a year after the end of the Civil War. A black workman, a businessman with his daughter, an old-time trapper, several others with their former uniform caps, suggest a substantial frontier outpost. This picture also demonstrates one particular aspect of the wood-engraving printing process. A full-page view such as this was generally drawn and engraved on nine small wood blocks that were screwed together before printing. Usually this was done so skillfully that the separate sections cannot be distinguished. In this view, particularly in the lower left, the edges of the blocks didn't join closely and the individual sections of the wood engraving are clearly outlined. (*Harper's Weekly*, July 28, 1866; William H. Merrick.) OPPOSITE: A Kansas land office in the 1870s. Prospective homesteaders review a sectional map of Sedgwick County on the wall in the background. For about half a century after this view was drawn, more and more of Kansas' virgin prairie was put under cultivation. Agricultural prosperity followed, but the unchecked plowing under of so much land contributed greatly to the devastating effects of the dust storms of the 1930s. (*Harper's Weekly*, July 11, 1874; Frenzeny and Tavernier.)

ABOVE: A cyclone ripping through the town of New Ulm, Minnesota, on July 16, 1881. While the Mennonites from Russia were settling in Kansas, emigrants from Germany, Sweden and Norway headed for Minnesota. Among Minnesota towns, New Ulm, on the Minnesota River in the southwestern part of the state, had a particularly violent history. In a hard-fought battle during the Sioux uprising of 1862, 190 buildings were burned and many settlers were killed, but eventually the Indians were driven off. Rebuilt, the town was devastated again by the storm pictured here. (*Frank Leslie's Illustrated Newspaper*, August 6, 1881.) OPPOSITE, TOP: A Mennonite religious service outside their barracks in central Kansas. More than 10,000 Mennonites, victims of religious persecution in czarist Russia, arrived in Kansas between 1874 and 1884. They brought trunks filled with carefully selected grains of drought-resistant Turkey Red wheat. The Russian wheat prospered on the Kansas prairie, and from that time on wheat became crucial to Kansas' economy. (*Frank Leslie's Illustrated Newspaper*, March 20, 1875.) OPPOSITE, BOTTOM: The interior of a huge barracks built by a colony of Russian Mennonites in central Kansas. As the Mennonites settled in, families built individual homes—prairie dugouts with thatched roofs at first, then log cabins and, after a while, substantial houses. Many descendants of these first Mennonite colonies are prosperous Kansas farmers today. (*Frank Leslie's Illustrated Newspaper*, March 20, 1875.)

The port city of Galveston (above) and a moonlit view of Houston. These two early Texas views were first published in 1845, the year in which the annexation of Texas by the United States was approved by the congresses of both the U.S. and Texas. Texas had won its independence from Mexico following Sam Houston's famous victory at San Jacinto on April 21, 1836. Houston had been Texas' first capital until being replaced by the city of Austin in 1839. These views were first published in England, where there was a lot of interest in Texas. The English government, in one of history's lost causes, had tried to oppose the annexation of Texas by the United States in an attempt to prevent the U.S. from expanding westward all the way to the Pacific. This English attempt at international politics backfired and helped swing sentiment in the U.S. in favor of the annexation. (*The Illustrated London News*, January 4, 1845.)

ABOVE: A steamboat on Houston's Buffalo Bayou in 1873. After a turbulent passage through the Civil War period, Texas was readmitted to the Union under a new constitution in 1869. The next decades were a period of unchecked growth for the huge state. With the Comanches settled on an Oklahoma reservation after 1874, farming in Texas prospered, fueled by immigration from every part of America and from Europe. The cattle industry boomed on the west Texas plains, and the spread of railroads as the century wore on made it increasingly feasible and profitable to ship Texas' beef and produce to markets around the country. (*Frank Leslie's Illustrated Newspaper*, June 28, 1873.) BELOW: Paris, Texas, on a market day in 1888. When this view was published, this north Texas farming town of 14,000 confidently expected to double its size before the end of the century. Paris used the pages of *Frank Leslie's* to invite readers in the North to come to Texas and build their futures growing corn and cotton on the rich and then still plentiful farmland of Lamar County. (*Frank Leslie's Illustrated Newspaper*, July 28, 1888.)

ABOVE: Covered wagons and the camps of recently arrived emigrants outside San Diego, California, in 1873. *Frank Leslie's* published this picture to celebrate the advantages of San Diego, which were already apparent when it was named the southern terminus of the Southern Pacific Railroad, then under construction. Though San Diego was then a town of only 2,000, the newspaper mentioned its incomparable climate, magnificent harbor and rich surrounding farmland as factors that would surely make it one of California's great cities. (*Frank Leslie's Illustrated Newspaper*, June 28, 1873.) BELOW: Astoria, Oregon, in 1868. Astoria had been founded in 1811 when John Jacob Astor, head of the Pacific Fur Company, sent an expedition of fur traders on a nine-month voyage around South America to establish a trading post near the mouth of the Columbia River. The Hudson's Bay Company and others were active in this fur-rich area in those years, but efforts to settle and farm the Pacific Northwest didn't

materialize until the 1830s and 1840s. The fur industry peaked before 1840, but Astoria survived as a trading post and port. (*Harper's Weekly*, May 30, 1868.) OPPOSITE: Two days of rain (January 18–19, 1886) brought a surprise flood to Los Angeles, California, where there was usually so little rainfall that no system of drainage or runoff ditches existed. Twenty-five homes were washed away, and the new station of the Los Angeles and San Gabriel Valley Railroad sailed off down the Los Angeles River, but only four people were drowned. The flood came at a time of great population growth for Los Angeles and southern California. The Gold Rush had made little impact on California south of Monterey, and as late as 1860 the population of the city of Los Angeles was only 1,600. However, the last decades of the century saw a vast influx of settlers that increased the population of Los Angeles County to over 100,000 by 1900. (*Frank Leslie's Illustrated Newspaper*, February 13, 1886; E. L. Merritt.)

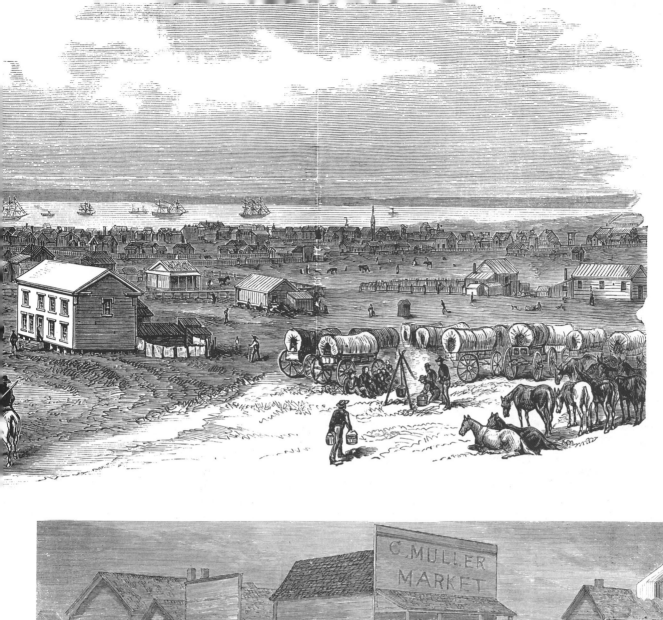

ABOVE: Saturday noon in an unnamed Southwestern town. Farmers, ranchers, hired hands and children are in town to shop, exchange gossip, entertain themselves and sell their produce. No details are given, but this may be a view of Denison, Texas, where *Harper's* artists Paul Frenzeny and Jules Tavernier stayed during their long Western tour in 1873–74. (*Harper's Weekly*, July 25, 1874; Frenzeny and Tavernier.) OPPOSITE, TOP: The home of Kit Carson in Taos, New Mexico. This illustration was sketched in 1860, some years after the legendary mountain man and trapper had retired to lead a quiet life with his family. The great frontiersman, who had made his reputation as a guide with John C. Frémont's exploring expeditions in the 1840s, was occupying his time, the *Frank Leslie's* correspondent reported, as a government agent for the Ute Indians. Carson's retirement proved not to be permanent. The following year saw him back in the field with the First New Mexico Volunteers on the Union side in the Civil War.

After the war Carson was made superintendent of Indian affairs for the Colorado Territory, a position he held when he died in 1868. (*Frank Leslie's Illustrated Newspaper*, December 8, 1860; A. D. Richardson.) OPPOSITE, BOTTOM: Santa Fe, New Mexico, at the end of the Civil War. The Spanish in Mexico established a provincial capital in Santa Fe as early as 1610. In 1821 William Becknell, a well-known Indian fighter and veteran of the War of 1812, left Missouri to establish a trade route 800 miles overland to Santa Fe. Becknell got there and returned, but passage through the territory of the Osage Indians proved perilous to many. Trade on the legendary Santa Fe Trail, which Becknell established, grew steadily in later decades. During the Mexican War, Santa Fe was occupied by American forces under the command of Gen. Stephen Watts Kearny. In 1851 the city became the capital of the Territory of New Mexico. (*Harper's Weekly*, April 21, 1866; Theodore R. Davis.)

F865 T55 1974

F591 .A4 1992

F614 .L58 F477 1990

OPPOSITE, TOP: Salt Lake City in 1858, 11 years after the first Mormons under Brigham Young reached the valley of the Great Salt Lake. Their goal had been to escape the violent religious conflicts in which they had been continually involved in the East, and to establish an isolated community that would be governed by the Church of Jesus Christ of Latter-Day Saints. After some difficult early years when food was scarce and crops were attacked by plagues of insects, the Mormon community in Utah grew and prospered. Bringing water from mountain streams by means of irrigation canals, they transformed the arid Salt Lake valley into productive farmland. In this view the foreground is dominated by the Deseret Store. (Deseret was a word for honeybee—signifying industry—found in the *Book of Mormon*. The Mormons originally wanted to call their state Deseret.) To this store, Salt Lake City's Mormons brought ten per cent of their produce as a tithe; it was then sold to raise funds for the church. The structure at the far right with the series of gabled windows was the home of Brigham Young and his many wives. (*Harper's Weekly*, September 4, 1858; based on a photograph by Burr & Mogo.) OPPOSITE, BOTTOM: A humorous drawing of a Mormon introducing his fifth wife to the rest of his already large family. This was a common subject for cartoon humor in the Eastern press during the years when the

Mormons in Utah practiced polygamy openly. In actuality, only 20% of Mormon men ever had more than one wife at a time, and two-thirds of those had only two. Brigham Young's 27 wives and 56 children were the exception. (*Harper's Weekly*, January 2, 1875; Frenzeny and Tavernier.) BELOW: A Mormon religious service in the famous Tabernacle. Ground was broken in 1853 for the great Mormon Temple in Salt Lake City. Designed by Truman O. Angell, following Brigham Young's vision, the huge granite structure was not completed until 1892. (*Harper's Weekly*, September 30, 1871.) BELOW, INSET: Brigham Young, who became leader of the Mormons after the 1844 murder of Joseph Smith by a mob in Carthage, Illinois. Young led several thousand Mormons who made the 1,400-mile trek on foot from Illinois to Utah in 1846–47. Hundreds died of cholera along the way. (*Harper's Weekly*, January 27, 1872.)

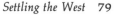

ABOVE: A wagon train at Helena, Montana Territory. Helena had been founded in 1862 by a group of prospectors down on their luck. When this view was drawn in 1878, it was a thriving frontier community of about 10,000. Helena's merchants received goods by wagon train either from Fort Benton, 75 miles away on the Missouri, or from Carrol, 250 miles farther down the Missouri near the mouth of the Mussel Shell. Reaching Helena from either of these outposts involved a dangerous overland journey through Sioux territory, but if the large wagon trains stayed close together they usually arrived safely. The view presents a fine panorama of town life on the frontier: the mounted prospector leading his well-packed mule down the main street past the Chinese worker and some friendly Indians while the wagon trains, some pulled by mules, others by oxen, are unpacked and reloaded for the return journey. (*Harper's Weekly*, February 2, 1878; W. M. Cary.) OPPO-SITE, TOP: The "Broadway" or main street of Yankton, Dakota Territory, in 1865, a few years after the town was established. Yankton and Vermillion, both settled in 1859, were the first permanent settlements in present-day South Dakota. (*Harper's*

Weekly, October 28, 1865; M. K. Armstrong.) OPPOSITE, BOTTOM: A busy scene on the Red River at Fargo, Dakota Territory, in 1878. The men at right are building the hull of a stern-wheel steamboat like the one in the distance. The Missouri River stern-wheelers were slower than the Mississippi's famous side-wheelers, but were designed for shallow water. They could carry 200 tons of freight in a waist-high river, and when unloaded needed only 20 inches of water in which to navigate. The tall structure on the riverbank is the grain elevator of the Grandin farm 40 miles to the north. Grain was brought overland from the farm to be shipped to the mill from Fargo, the highest point on the river that steam-powered boats could reach. In the foreground, a local land agent is showing maps of the region to a family of newly arrived immigrants. Settlement of the region boomed in the 1870s after the railroad reached the Red River from St. Paul and Duluth, Minnesota. North Dakota quickly became one of the great wheat-growing centers of the nation. North and South Dakota both achieved statehood on November 2, 1889. (*Harper's Weekly*, August 27, 1881; W. A. Rogers.)

OPPOSITE: A group of Oklahoma Boomers (would-be settlers) being ejected by the Army from the Indian Territory in 1885. In that year, several companies of black soldiers of the Ninth Cavalry were in the field trying to restrain the Oklahoma Boomers. (*Harper's Weekly*, March 28, 1885; T. de Thulstrup, based on a sketch by Frederic Remington.) ABOVE: A wagon train of settlers who had hoped to claim land in Oklahoma leaving Arkansas City, Kansas, in 1885, and abandoning their plans to invade what was then still the Indian Territory. In 1828 Congress had reserved Oklahoma for the Indians, requiring all white settlers to leave. Eventually, more than 60 tribes were settled there. The name Oklahoma derives from Choctaw words meaning "red people." During the Civil War, the leaders of the Five Civilized Tribes—Cherokee, Choctaw, Chickasaw, Creek and Seminole—which had come from Southern states, allied themselves with the Con-

federacy. Oklahoma then became a battleground, and suffered the penalties of the defeated during the Reconstruction Era. The federal government had little interest in defending the borders of the Indians in Oklahoma who had opposed them in the Civil War. Some Oklahoma territory was given to former slaves, additional tribes were brought in, whether there was room for them or not, and railroads were granted access to what had once been the exclusive domain of the Indians. Pressure to open the Territory to white settlement increased. By the late 1870s organized bands of hopeful settlers were continually trespassing within the borders of Oklahoma. Many were ejected, and some, like those pictured here, were convinced not to try and headed off for points unknown. Within a few years, the settlers were finally allowed in, and the great Oklahoma land rush followed. (*Frank Leslie's Illustrated Newspaper*, May 16, 1885.)

ABOVE: The line outside the land office in Guthrie, Oklahoma, on April 22, 1889. On this day Congress, bowing to the inevitable, opened the first two million acres of the western part of the Indian Territory to settlement by non-Indian homesteaders. At noon on April 22, at least 100,000 would-be settlers rushed across the neighboring borders of Kansas, Texas and Arkansas to claim land. Many of course tried to get a head start, and many of these were ejected by the Cavalry in the days before April 22. Some succeeded in evading the Cavalry and getting to some of the good claims *sooner* than the others, whence the future state's nickname. Guthrie, Oklahoma, *Harper's* pointed out, was, unlike Rome, built in a day. At nightfall on April 21 its population was zero; 24 hours later its population was 10,000. Streets had been laid out, lots had been staked off, a municipal government formed. Later land rushes periodically opened more and more of the former Indian Territory to settlement. Statehood for Oklahoma followed in 1907 after the various Indian tribes had been assigned to specific areas by the federal government, and had approved the proposed constitution of the new state. (*Harper's Weekly*, May 18, 1889.)
BELOW: The main street of Purcell, Oklahoma, very shortly after the 1889 land rush. (*Frank Leslie's Illustrated Newspaper*, April 27, 1889.)

ABOVE: Settlers in Oklahoma laying out a town near Guthrie in the first days after April 22, 1889. Everyone lived in tents until permanent homes could be built. The crucial task of the early days was to establish local governments that could both maintain law and order and begin to register the thousands of land claims that settlers were eager to file. Guthrie was the business center of the region because of its position on the line of the Santa Fe, which had been allowed to lay its tracks through the Indian Territory long before 1889. (*Frank Leslie's Illustrated Newspaper*, May 1, 1889; from a photograph by C. E. De Groff.) BELOW: A sprawling view of Oklahoma City a few weeks after April 22. (*Harper's Weekly*, May 18, 1889; based on photographs.)

ABOVE: In a Western vigilante court, the noose is being hung over the telegraph pole for the three miscreants with their hands tied in the left foreground. The bearded man at right was injured during the chase. (*Harper's Weekly*, April 11, 1874; Frenzeny and Tavernier.) OPPOSITE, TOP: *Harper's* and *Leslie's* as a rule hardly covered the news of Western outlaws and lawmen, but April 1882 saw a story so big that it couldn't be ignored. The notorious Jesse James had been shot and killed in St. Joseph, Missouri, by Robert Ford, a member of his own gang. Ford was after a $10,000 reward being offered for James and his brother Frank, dead or alive, by Missouri's governor, Thomas T. Crittenden. This view shows the house where the killing occurred on April 3. Crowds gathered to see the scene where the famous outlaw had met his end. Born in Missouri in 1847, James fought for the South in the Civil War with "Bloody" Bill Anderson's guerrillas. Shot and wounded by federal soldiers in an incident after the war was officially over, James turned to a life of crime. For the next 16 years, he and his gang robbed stores, stagecoaches, banks and trains. In one of their most famous robberies, James's gang was decimated at Northfield,

Minnesota, on September 7, 1876, when trying to rob the First National Bank. Of the eight gang members, only Frank and Jesse James escaped being caught or killed. After Jesse was killed, Frank surrendered. Tried and acquitted, he lived the rest of his life on a quiet Missouri farm. (*Frank Leslie's Illustrated Newspaper*, April 15, 1882.) OPPOSITE, BOTTOM: Vigilante justice accompanied the establishment of farms, towns and ranches throughout the West. In some areas vigilante groups were comprised of local farmers, merchants and ranchers who took the law into their own hands in order to provide some sort of authority where there was none. They defended their communities as fairly as they could. In other areas criminals plundered the countryside under the mask of vigilante action. Certainly the system lent itself to widespread abuse, but accounts that reached the Eastern press in the nineteenth century generally praised those who proclaimed themselves on the side of law and order. Here a Texas vigilante court is about to execute a member of a gang that had shot up a saloon in a dispute over a prisoner taken by the local sheriff. (*Frank Leslie's Illustrated Newspaper*, November 12, 1881.)

OPPOSITE: A two-man weather station at Fort Gibson in the Indian Territory. Similar stations had also been established at Pike's Peak, Denver and Santa Fe as the federal government began the practice of tracking weather, which generally moves west to east across the United States. Weather prediction was a science then in its infancy, but wind, temperature and atmospheric-pressure readings were taken at these little stations and sent East by telegraph. *Harper's* reported that the Indian Territory station was once attacked after a long storm by the local Cherokee, who thought it was exercising a malignant influence over the weather. The Indians were finally, if reluctantly, persuaded to abandon the assault when the purpose of the station was carefully explained. (*Harper's Weekly*, March 21, 1874; Frenzeny and Tavernier.)
ABOVE: A government surveying party in Colorado in the 1870s. Surveying and mapping the immense area covered by Western states and territories was a huge undertaking, and one that was hardly completed before the closing of the frontier. Trains of pack mules took surveyors into remote areas where wagons couldn't go. A pack mule could carry 200 pounds of supplies and was a valuable commodity on the frontier. (*Harper's Weekly*, October 12, 1878; I. P. Pranishnikoff.)

ABOVE: One of John Butterfield's Overland stagecoaches attacked by Indians on the plains in 1866. *Harper's* artist Theodore R. Davis experienced this attack firsthand. He and his traveling companions survived unwounded, but in later years they could recall the grisly experience of finding many mutilated corpses on the plains during this period of Indian unrest. He and his small traveling party chased away the wolves and buried the bodies as well as they could before moving on. A journey by stagecoach in the 1860s was certain to be uncomfortable, and could often be harrowing. In 1857 Congress granted John Butterfield a $600,000 annual subsidy to establish a mail and passenger stagecoach service from Missouri to the Pacific. Later that year Butterfield inaugurated service on the famous "oxbow" route, 2,630 miles from Tipton, Missouri, via El Paso and Tucson to Los Angeles, and up the California coast to San Francisco. Departures were twice weekly each way, and the goal was to cover the route in 25 days. The Overland Mail, as the service was called, carried a letter for ten cents and took a passenger over the entire route for $200. Butterfield got relatively few through passengers, but sold many short-haul tickets. He had 250 stagecoaches and wagons, employed 800 men, and kept 1,000 horses and 500 mules busy. The original route was in use until March 1861, when the start of the Civil War forced the company to adopt a more central route. (*Harper's Weekly*, April 21, 1866; Theodore R. Davis.) OPPOSITE, TOP: An Overland Mail coach crossing the Rocky Mountains in a snowstorm. This illustration was published early in 1868 when the Union Pacific and Central Pacific railroads were laying the tracks that the following year would be joined at Promontory to create the first transcontinental railroad. The Butterfield stages were still in use at this time, carrying passengers and mail between the completed sections of each railroad. (*Harper's Weekly*, February 8, 1868; Theodore R. Davis.) OPPOSITE, BOTTOM: The original title of this illustration told the whole story, "The Missing Mail—An Incident of the Plains." (*Harper's Weekly*, April 23, 1881.)

BELOW: The Overland coach office at Denver in 1866. Denver was the center of the Rocky Mountain mining area and had prospered since the first days of the Pike's Peak Gold Rush in the late 1850s. When this illustration was published in January 1866, any traveler from coast to coast still had to cover 2,000 miles by stage. The Eastern railroad had barely reached Atchison, Kansas, and the Central Pacific was no farther than Placerville, California. It took five days from Atchison to Denver, and at least another 12 days to Placerville. (*Harper's Weekly*, January 27, 1866; Theodore R. Davis.) OPPOSITE, TOP: An Overland Mail coach setting out from Atchison, Kansas, in 1866. The coaches were notoriously uncomfortable. Each passenger had about 15 inches of sitting room, the roads were bumpy and the sleepless passengers were quickly covered with alkali dust. Each passenger was allowed 25 pounds of luggage, two blankets and a canteen. Food provided at stations along the way was primitive. A coach could carry about five passengers at a time. The goal, on flat land, was to cover 100 miles every 24 hours. The goal in the mountains was just to get across. (*Harper's Weekly*, January 27, 1866; William H. Merrick.) OPPOSITE, BOTTOM: An Overland Mail coach starting out from San Francisco in 1858. This illustration was based on a photograph that must have been taken on a ceremonial occasion. The six horses couldn't have pulled this coach very far with a driver and 12 passengers perched on top as well as a full load inside. (*Harper's Weekly*, December 11, 1858.)

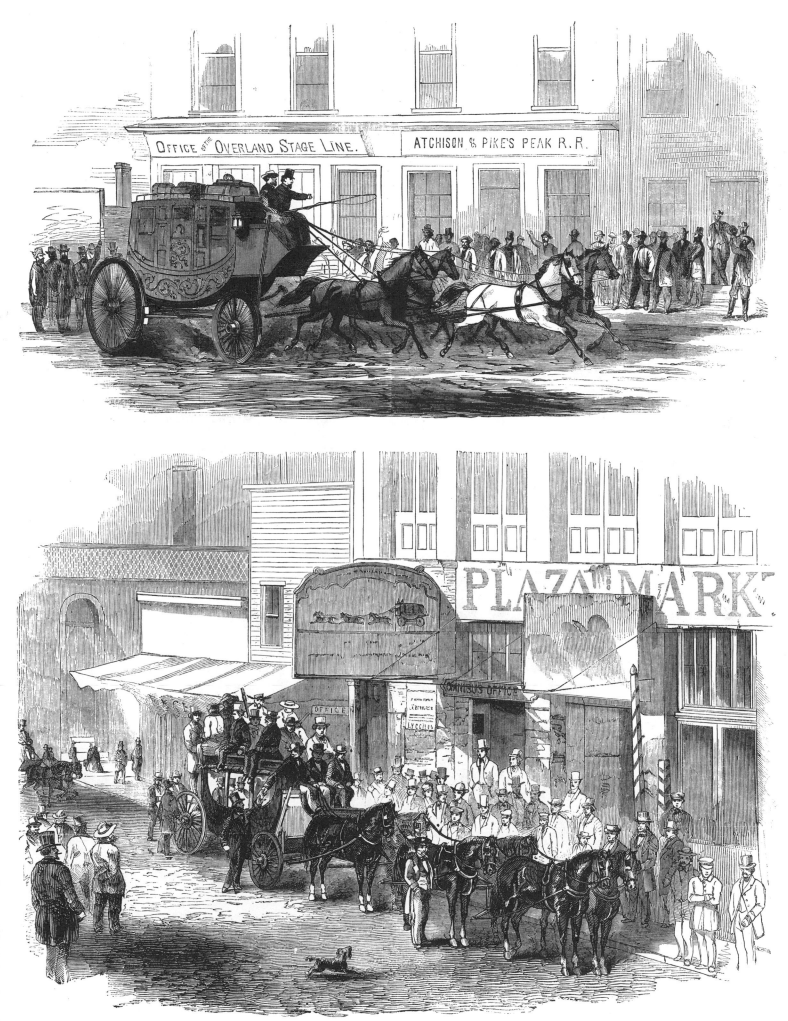

LEFT: A Western stagecoach going all out. It took great skill to drive a stagecoach, holding three pairs of reins in one hand and the whip in the other. Drivers were famous for being cantankerous, profane, self-reliant individuals who could deal with Indians, floods, sandstorms and robbers and still get through with mail, passengers and often a strongbox weighing 100 pounds intact. The great Concord coaches, built in Concord, New Hampshire, were about eight and a half feet long and eight feet high, weighed 2,500 pounds and cost about $1,300 when the Overland Mail was in operation. Butterfield had to spend about $1 million to get his operation going, but he had the guaranteed government subsidy of $600,000 for six years to see him through. Other operators, without such subsidies, usually found they couldn't make a profit with the cost of coaches, horses, building stations, hiring men, etc. Horses on the Butterfield route did about 15 miles before being changed. (*Frank Leslie's Illustrated Newspaper*, January 25, 1890; Jerome H. Smith.) OPPOSITE, TOP: A Nevada stagecoach in 1890. (*Harper's Weekly*, March 22, 1890; H. F. Farny.) OPPOSITE, BOTTOM: With the stagecoach came the stagecoach robbery. Here an Eastern dude is being stripped of his valuables by some rough-looking customers near Leadville, Colorado, in the early 1880s. (*Frank Leslie's Illustrated Newspaper*, November 11, 1882.)

OPPOSITE, TOP: The history of Western transportation had some unusual byways. Soldiers at Fort Kearney were startled one night in 1860 when some eager Pike's Peakers came sailing over the horizon in this wind-powered wagon. It had two sails and a lamp rigged in front for night driving. (*Frank Leslie's Illustrated Newspaper*, July 7, 1860.) OPPOSITE, BOTTOM: A camel train in Nevada's mining country in the 1870s. In 1855, with the backing of Secretary of War Jefferson Davis, Congress approved funds to bring a small, experimental number of camels to America to test their usefulness for military and other purposes. Two shipments, totaling fewer than 100 animals, arrived in 1856 and 1857, and the camels were stationed near San Antonio, Texas. In 1857 a 25-camel caravan successfully completed a four-month journey from San Antonio to Los Angeles under specially hired Turkish, Greek and Armenian camel drivers. After that first test, however, official interest in the camel waned, and the Civil War intervened to end the project forever. Some of the camels in government hands were stationed for a time at Western Army forts, but most were auctioned off. Some of these found their way into circuses; others were used by private freight-hauling and road-construction outfits. Many were eventually abandoned on the desert to fend for themselves. Stories of camels turning up unexpectedly at odd places persisted until the turn of the century. (*Harper's Weekly*, June 30, 1877; Paul Frenzeny.) ABOVE: A Pony Express rider. This engraving is after a painting by George Ottinger, an early Utah artist and partner in the pioneer firm of Western photographers, Savage and Ottinger of Salt Lake City. The scene is near Nebraska's Chimney Rock. It shows the rider passing workmen erecting the first transcontinental telegraph. The completion of the telegraph in the fall of 1861 would spell the end of the legendary Pony Express after a brief, but action-packed 18-month

career. In 1859 the staging firm of Russell, Majors & Waddell undertook to establish a fast overland mail service between St. Joseph, Missouri, and Sacramento, California, that would use riders on horseback rather than the much slower stagecoaches already running on the Butterfield line. The Pony Express route was 1,966 miles long. The operation required the expenditure of over $100,000 just to begin. Five hundred fast horses had to be purchased, 80 riders hired and 190 stations (many at first just a tent on the prairie) had to be built. On April 3, 1860, riders set out from both ends of the route. At first the trips required about ten and a half days, compared to the 23–25 days that the Butterfield stages took on their more southerly, longer route. Eventually the Pony Express got its time down to about eight days. Horses were changed at each station, about ten miles apart. A rider covered about 75 miles before passing the mail to the next man. From Sacramento to San Francisco, mail was carried by steamer down the Sacramento River. On the first run both horse and rider were put on the boat so that a welcoming crowd could greet the first Pony Express rider and his somewhat seasick horse as they proceeded from San Francisco's Embarcadero to Portsmouth Square. In 18 months the Pony Express carried 34,753 pieces of mail at a cost of between $2 and $10 an ounce, but the service never came close to making a profit. Expenses were high; hostile Indians and bad weather took their toll on riders, horses and stations; and hoped-for government subsidies were not forthcoming. The completion of the telegraph made the Pony Express unnecessary, and it was discontinued a few days after the first messages went out over the new wires. (*Harper's Weekly*, November 2, 1867; from a photograph by Savage and Ottinger of a painting by George Ottinger.)

A late train bent on making up lost time flying out of the Western mountains. (*Harper's Weekly*, August 30, 1890; Charles Graham.)

The Railroads

THE BUILDING OF THE FIRST transcontinental railroad in the 1860s was one of the great engineering feats in American history. The dream of building a railroad to the West began with the Gold Rush. In 1853 Congress appropriated $150,000 to survey possible routes. The Army Engineers explored five possible routes spread out across the country from north to south. One of the strongest advocates of a railroad to the Pacific was Secretary of War Jefferson Davis. Coming from Mississippi, Davis pushed hard for a southern route, but the beginning of the Civil War in 1861, before the final decision had been made, ended any chance of that. The routes chosen for exploration in the 1850s, however, were selected in Washington for political reasons, and none proved ideal. It was finally found that the eastern part of the line, from Nebraska to the Rockies, could hardly do better than to more or less follow the route of the Oregon Trail.

While the initial political skirmishing over the transcontinental route was going on, the need for a line to the Pacific was becoming increasingly obvious. So many people were traveling to California via Panama that by the middle of the 1850s the Panama Railroad was completed to accommodate them. Crossing the 48-mile-wide isthmus between Aspinwall (now Colón) on the Atlantic and Panama City on the Pacific, the Panama Railroad carried 200,000 passengers in its first four years, from 1855 to 1859. One-way fare was $25. It wasn't lost on some American businessmen that there were huge profits to be made completing a line from coast to coast.

A major obstacle to the American transcontinental railroad was conquered, at least on paper, at the end of the 1850s. A brilliant young engineer named Theodore Dehone Judah mapped a workable, if difficult, route through the Sierra via Donner Pass. Judah's route would require building 15 tunnels, six up the western slope of the Sierra, nine down the other side, but it was feasible, given sufficient financing. Judah went to four successful California businessmen, Leland Stanford, Charles Crocker, Mark Hopkins and Collis P. Huntington. A persuasive man, Judah interested the four hardheaded entrepreneurs, not by visions of a ribbon of steel from coast to coast, but by practical talk about the profits they could make supplying the Nevada mining camps near which their line would pass. As the Big Four, as they came to be known, had all made their money as merchants in the Gold Rush, this was an argument they could understand. In 1861 the Central Pacific Railroad was incorporated with Judah as its chief engineer. The Big Four ultimately turned rather modest initial investments, not more than $150,000 total, into vast personal fortunes. Judah didn't live to see his dreams realized; he contracted yellow fever on a trip East via Panama and died in 1863.

Abraham Lincoln signed the Pacific Railroad Act into law on July 1, 1862. The Act authorized the Central Pacific to build tracks east from Sacramento, and the Union Pacific to build west from Omaha, Nebraska. Each line was to get a 400-foot-wide strip of land on which to build, plus ten alternating square-mile sections of public land for each mile of track. The railroads, and this was crucial, would receive government loan bonds at low interest, repayable in 30 years. The loans would be $16,000 for each mile of track on flat land, $32,000 for each mile in the deserts of Utah and Nevada and $48,000 for each mile in the mountains. Two years later, while the railroads were just getting started, the land grants were doubled and the loan terms were liberalized. The original plan was that the lines would meet at the California/Nevada border, but an 1866 ruling made it a contest. Each railroad was authorized to build as far and as fast as it could. The two railroads eventually received 21 million acres of public land, an area about equal to Connecticut, Vermont and Massachusetts combined. They sold most of it to homesteaders at the going rate of $2.50 an acre. (The government similarly sold the sections they retained.)

In subsequent decades other railroads received similar land grants that ultimately reached a total of 131 million acres. In return, for decades the federal government received discounts of about 50% on all of its traffic—mail, freight and troops. The value of these discounts over the years far surpassed the value of the land at the time it was given away.

Where the government and the public were not so well served was in the construction of the railroad itself. The organizers of the Union Pacific were led by Thomas C. Durant, a wily and politically well-connected financier, in some ways the epitome of the robber baron. They secretly formed a construction company, the Credit Mobilier, and in effect hired themselves to build the railroad at hugely inflated fees that would be paid with the federal government's loan bonds. The Central Pacific's Big Four did much the same with an organization called the Contract and Finance Company.

The Central Pacific broke ground on January 8, 1863, at Sacramento, but in the early years literally inched its way toward the mountains. The Union Pacific wasn't much faster. The line was 40 miles west of Omaha by the end of 1865, 265 miles farther along by the end of 1866. Both lines faced difficulties. For the Union Pacific, one of its greatest problems was the need for lumber for ties. There was no timber on the plains, and all of the wood had to be brought from Wisconsin. The Central Pacific had plenty of lumber, but no local heavy-metal industry to call on. All of its rails, spikes and other metal parts had to be brought around South America by sea from Eastern factories. Labor was also scarce in California, so Crocker hit on the idea of importing Chinese workers. The Union Pacific used mostly Irish immigrants. By the peak winter of 1868–69 the railroads were jointly employing about 25,000 workers. It was an immense logistical undertaking, requiring 40 railroad cars full of material to lay just one mile of track. Each mile took 400 sections of rail weighing 700 pounds each, 2,400 wooden ties (slightly more if the terrain wasn't level), 4,000 iron spikes, etc. When he wrote his memoirs after the turn of the century, the Union Pacific's chief engineer, Grenville M. Dodge, recalled with pardonable pride that the work had never been delayed for any significant period of time by the absence of the necessary materials.

In the late spring of 1869 it appeared that the two lines might not actually meet as competing grading crews worked past each other in the Utah desert. With federal intervention, the little town of Promontory, 70 miles northwest of Salt Lake City, was selected as the meeting point. The day for the joining of the rails was supposed to be May 8, but Durant was delayed en route to the ceremonies for two days in a dispute with some tie cutters who kidnapped him in Piedmont, Wyoming, because their wages had not been paid in several months. Durant wired for the funds, and was released in time to reach Promontory on May 10. At the historic ceremony, Stanford was handed a special silver maul with which to drive in the famous golden last spike. He swung at it and missed, and handed the maul to Durant who, ever the politician, politely missed also. Nevertheless, a telegrapher on the scene sent the simple message "Done," setting off celebrations from coast to coast. Where the tracks joined at Promontory, the Union Pacific had laid 1,086 miles of track west from its hub at Omaha. The Central Pacific, with the more difficult mountains to conquer, had laid 689 miles east from Sacramento. For many the spirit of the occasion was best captured by the opening lines of Bret Harte's famous poem:

> What was it the engines said,
> Pilots touching head to head,
> Facing on a single track,
> Half a world behind each back?

PRECEDING PAGES: The greatest moment in the history of American railroading: the joining of the rails at Promontory, Utah, on May 10, 1869. In the background are the two locomotives—*Jupiter* of the Central Pacific (on the left) and *No. 119* of the Union Pacific—that stood 30 feet apart while the ceremonial last spike was driven, and then were moved into position to touch each other as workmen proposed suitable toasts. In the center, S. S. Montague (left) of the Central Pacific is shaking hands with Grenville M. Dodge of the Union Pacific. A trip from coast to coast could now be completed in eight days instead of months by sea or overland by wagon train. (*Frank Leslie's Illustrated Newspaper*, June 5, 1869; based on a photograph by A. J. Russell.) ABOVE: *Harper's* published this view of a typical railroad-building scene on the Great Plains in 1875, six years after the joining of the rails at Promontory. In this view the construction train has pulled up to within a few feet of where workmen are completing the track. A section of rail is being lowered into position while ties are being driven securely into the ground. Supplies for the workmen are being delivered from the nearest town or trading post in a convoy of small covered wagons. Smaller flatbed wagons are bringing in loads of wooden ties, probably from a freight car of the construction train, and heading back for more. Supply trains such as the one pictured here carried not only the ties, rails and spikes needed to lay the track, but included carpenter shops, machine shops, food supplies, kitchens, offices, general stores, water supplies and sleeping accommodations. In the first years of construction, the Union Pacific completed about a mile of track per day, later speeding up to two to three miles a day. Railroad building required teamwork and planning. First, surveyors plotted the general route. Next, location men staked out exact grades and curves. Grading crews then made the ground ready for the tracks. Finally, the tracklayers put down the rails. Bridge-building crews worked at least a few miles ahead of the tracklayers. Isolated bridge-building, surveying and tie-cutting crews sometimes found themselves vulnerable to Indian attack. In 1868–69 a few thousand soldiers patrolled the Union Pacific line across the plains to defend the workmen from assaults by the Sioux and Cheyenne. The Central Pacific had no problem with Indians. (*Harper's Weekly*, July 17, 1875; A. R. Waud.) OPPOSITE: A Central Pacific train, powered by dual locomotives as was commonly done in the mountains. This illustration was drawn for *Frank Leslie's* during the paper's 1878 transcontinental tour when a large party of Easterners made the round trip to California. As the excursion train rounded this bend, passengers could look down the mountain to the South Fork of the American River where gold had been discovered in 1848. In the high Sierra, the Central Pacific's track reached an elevation of 7,017 feet above sea level. After climbing to the summit, the train could coast down the mountains largely without power. (*Frank Leslie's Illustrated Newspaper*, April 27, 1878.)

OPPOSITE, TOP: A Union Pacific train heading east from Cheyenne, Wyoming, attacked by Indians on June 14, 1870, a year after the transcontinental railroad had been completed. In this incident no passengers were injured and the train was undamaged, but several of the Indians' horses were killed. The engraving was based on a sketch made by a passenger. (*Frank Leslie's Illustrated Newspaper*, July 9, 1870.) OPPOSITE, BOTTOM: Joseph Becker, a *Frank Leslie's* staff artist, made a rail trip across America in October 1869. In subsequent months he published several drawings based on what he saw and heard along the way. In a little town near the Platte River, Becker heard the story of a party of Union Pacific workmen whose handcar was attacked by Indians. As the car was driven furiously toward a nearby station, some of the workmen returned fire, killing at least one of their assailants, and the Indians eventually withdrew. (*Frank Leslie's Illustrated Newspaper*,

March 26, 1870; Albert Berghaus, based on a sketch by Joseph Becker.) ABOVE: A train on the Kansas–Pacific line is shown here stopped near Kit Carson, Colorado. Passengers amuse themselves shooting at a small herd of pronghorn. When this sketch was published in 1875, *Harper's* reported that laws against this kind of aimless shooting were being more strictly enforced. In the early years of Western railroading, herds of animals on the tracks were one of the three major causes of accidents. The others were poorly laid track and overheated axle bearings, or "hot boxes" as they were known to the nineteenth-century railroader. But those weren't the only hazards. In 1874 a Union Pacific train was stopped at Kearney, Nebraska, by a solid three-foot-high wall of grasshoppers. (*Harper's Weekly*, May 29, 1875; Frenzeny and Tavernier.)

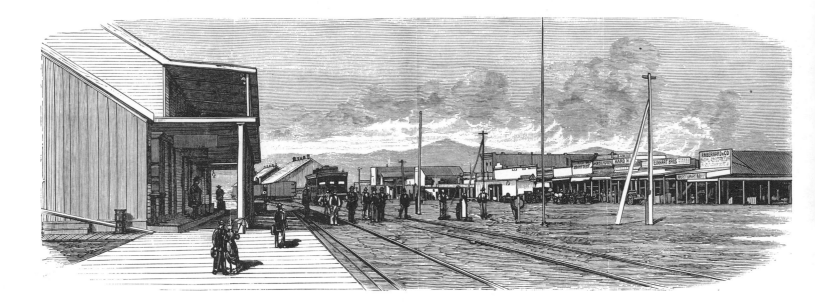

OPPOSITE, TOP: The railroad depot and main commercial street of the little town of Elko, Nevada, visited by the *Frank Leslie's* excursion train in 1878. Elko, in the Humboldt Desert, had mineral springs that promised future tourist business, and was near several mining centers that always desperately needed railroads to bring in supplies and carry away the gold or silver they produced. (*Frank Leslie's Illustrated Newspaper*, January 5, 1878.)
OPPOSITE, BOTTOM: A teeming station on the Union Pacific in 1869. Indians, an old-time hunter, soldiers, families of immigrants from Europe traveling to their new homes, a Chinese laborer on his way to his next job, hopeful prospectors, speculators, investors, gamblers—the whole panoply of Western humanity—are seen jostling each other in front of the station hotel, a tent in this case, promising square meals and lodging. Regular train service on the new transcontinental railroad began on May 15, 1869. Average time coast to coast was eight to ten days, depending on the weather. In first-class sleeping cars, the fare was $100 plus $4 a day. Second-class coaches were $75. Immigrants heading West paid about $40 for board seats and few comforts. Trains averaged about 20 miles per hour. With more than 200 stations and water stops along the route, these early passengers could hardly have had the sensation of continuous motion. (*Frank Leslie's Illustrated Newspaper*, December 11, 1869; Paul Frenzel.) ABOVE: A large water tank and windmill at Laramie, Wyoming Territory, used to refill the water tanks of locomotives on the Union Pacific. Through a self-regulating device, the windmill was activated to refill the large tank from a well when the water fell below a certain level. When the water level in the large tank was high enough, the windmill automatically shut down. *Frank Leslie's* reported that the windmill was 75 feet high and that the whole apparatus cost $10,000. (*Frank Leslie's Illustrated Newspaper*, May 8, 1869; based on a photograph by A. J. Russell.)

ABOVE: An elegantly appointed dining car on the Union Pacific in a picture published a few weeks after the transcontinental railroad was completed. Passengers paying lower fares had to find what food they could at stations along the way; by all accounts, it was uniformly terrible. (*Harper's Weekly*, May 29, 1869; A. R. Waud.) OPPOSITE, TOP: One of the hazards of the early days of Western railroading—a train overtaken by the floods that devastated southwestern Kansas in early May 1877, bringing travel to a standstill for several days. This train was overtaken by the flood near Emporia, Kansas. Its passengers were taken off on log rafts and small boats. (*Frank Leslie's Illustrated Newspaper*, June 16, 1877; T.

G. Rowan.) OPPOSITE, BOTTOM: Chinese laborers on the Central Pacific mingle with Irish workers on the Union Pacific as some final blasting is done preparatory to laying the last mile of track before the two lines joined on May 10, 1869. Laborers on the Union Pacific and Central Pacific earned about $35 a month in 1868–69. Defections every payday were a serious problem for management. As the railroad-building camps moved across the country, makeshift towns of gamblers, thieves and prostitutes moved with them. From this phenomenon the expression "hell on wheels" entered the language. (*Harper's Weekly*, May 29, 1869; A. R. Waud.)

THE SNOW PLOUGH AT WORK

OPPOSITE: A new invention, a rotary snowplow, on the Central Pacific in 1883. The rotary plow was more powerful than earlier plows, but snow was so deep at times in the Sierra Nevada and Rocky Mountains that shoveling by large crews of workmen was the only way to clear the tracks. Often workers could only find where the tracks were by the position of the telegraph lines that followed them. When a train was stuck in the snow, the first step was to back it up onto a siding so that the plows could get through. The snow blockades would be attacked from both ends if equipment was available. If the snow didn't yield to the plows, then crews were assembled to shovel their way out. Passengers were often so bored waiting for the tracks to be cleared that they readily joined in the work. (*Harper's Weekly*, February 1, 1890; Charles Graham.) ABOVE: A huge snowplow, pushed by two engines, at work on a Minnesota railroad in 1883. It was not unknown for passengers in the early days of Western railroading to be stuck for so long in the snow that they set out on foot to try to find food and shelter on a nearby farm or town; some froze to death in the attempt. (*Harper's Weekly*, January 27, 1883; Charles Graham.) RIGHT: Snowsheds on the Central Pacific during the difficult winter of 1871–72. In high snow and avalanche areas the Central Pacific built 37 miles of snowsheds, using 65 million board feet of lumber, at a cost of $10,000 to $30,000 per mile. The sheds were built to keep snow off areas of track particularly susceptible to drifts. The sheds worked well except that in the early years they were routinely set on fire by sparks from trains passing through, and workmen had to be stationed along the route to put the fires out. Later on, with improved plows and concrete sheds replacing some of the wooden ones, fewer workers were needed. *Harper's* reported that conditions were so bad in 1872 that one train took 20 days, three to four times longer than usual, to reach Chicago from San Francisco. (*Harper's Weekly*, February 10, 1872.)

OPPOSITE: *Harper's* reported that it cost the Denver and Rio Grande Railroad $140,000 a mile to build this narrow-gauge line through the canyon of the Río de las Animas, or River of Souls, near the new mining center of Silverton, Colorado. Standard-gauge railroads had tracks 4'8½" apart. Narrow-gauge lines with tracks just three feet apart were frequently built in inaccessible mountain areas, and added their own romantic chapter to the early days of Western railroading. Often two engines pulled trains thousands of feet above sea level in areas that a few years before had been accessible only to prospectors and their mules. With Denver as the hub, a network of narrow-gauge lines was painstakingly carved out of the Rockies. Profits from being the connecting link to civilization for new mining areas such as Leadville made it worthwhile. (*Harper's Weekly*, September 25, 1886; R. Schelling, based on a photograph by W. H. Jackson.)

ABOVE: The Dale Creek Bridge, Colorado, one of the engineering marvels of the Union Pacific. The bridge was 125 feet high and 500 feet long, a huge puzzle built of timber, all of which was brought to the site from Chicago, 1,000 miles to the east. (*The Illustrated London News*, November 27, 1869; based on a photograph by A. J. Russell.)

TOP, LEFT: The daughter of a Western postmaster poised to flag down a passing train with the mail. At isolated little stations, engineers wouldn't bother to stop if they didn't see anyone waiting. (*Harper's Weekly*, September 4, 1875; F. S. Church.) BOTTOM, LEFT: Workmen on a handcar riding down a mountain line to pick up new provisions for a crew high in the hills behind them. The return trip was much harder work. As everywhere in the West, telegraph lines may be seen following the tracks in the background. (*Harper's Weekly*, August 3, 1889; H. F. Farny, based on a sketch by Alfred Mitchell.) OPPOSITE, TOP: The ceremony at Gold Creek, Montana, on September 8, 1883, as the last spike is driven to complete the Northern Pacific, the nation's second transcontinental railroad. The line's president, Henry Villard, hammers the spike while in the background workmen sit on top of a sign giving the distance east to Lake Superior (1,198 miles) and west to Puget Sound (847 miles). The Northern Pacific, between Duluth, Minnesota, and Portland, Oregon, was created in 1864 by a bill signed by Abraham Lincoln, and took 19 years to complete. The 1873 financial panic brought the line's progress to a halt before Villard, who took over in 1881, saw it to completion. Crossing the Rockies farther north than the Central Pacific brought tremendous challenges, including blasting one tunnel 3,850 feet long out of solid granite. When completed, a round trip from the Mississippi River to the Columbia River could be made in nine days. The Southern Pacific, connecting New Orleans and Los Angeles, was also completed in 1883. Two years later the Atchison, Topeka and Santa Fe linked Chicago and southern California. The nation's fifth transcontinental line, the Great Northern, was finished in 1893. (*Harper's Weekly*, September 22, 1883; Schell and Hogan, from a sketch by Charles Graham.) OPPOSITE, BOTTOM: Western travel after the era of the wagon train. *Harper's* gave this picture the title "The Modern Ship of the Plains." The passengers reflect the boredom of long hours spent crossing the empty prairie, boredom that would only be compounded if heavy snows or floods added days or weeks to an already long trip. Immigrant passengers and others paying low fares were also always susceptible to being "switched off," having their trains shunted onto a siding so faster, more lucrative trains could pass. (*Harper's Weekly*, November 13, 1886; R. F. Zogbaum.)

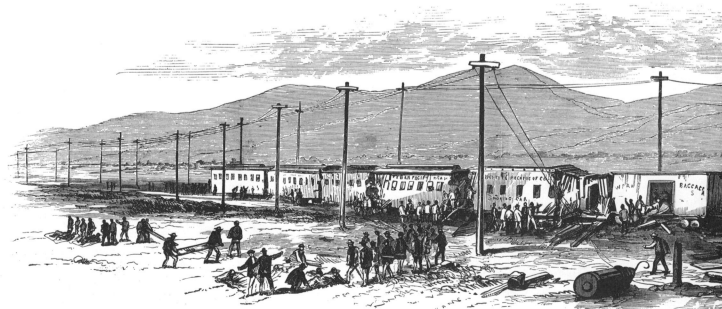

OPPOSITE, TOP: Thirteen people were killed and many injured in this Southern Pacific rail disaster on January 19, 1883, at the remote Tehachapi Pass, 100 miles northeast of Los Angeles in the lower Sierra Nevada Mountains. The train had stopped at the top of a steep grade to detach an extra engine, when the rest of the train began to slip back down the mountain. As the train gathered momentum, the first two cars broke free and made the descent safely. The larger part of the train, however, built up too much speed, crashed and burned. Two unidentified men who had been seen at the station were found in the wreck. Authorities theorized that they had disconnected the hand brakes to try to take the mail and freight cars down the mountain to rob them, but had then lost control of the train. (*Frank Leslie's Illustrated Newspaper*, February 3, 1883.) ABOVE: The railroad station at Lathrop, California, 80 miles east of San Francisco, the junction of the Southern and Central Pacific lines. (*Frank Leslie's Illustrated Newspaper*, May 11, 1878.) BELOW: *Frank Leslie's* described this as the first rail collision in California history. The accident occurred near Alameda on November 14, 1869, when an Alameda and San Francisco Railroad train crashed head-on into a Western Pacific train. There was a stretch of four miles where the two lines used the same track. The Western Pacific engineer received an erroneous verbal assurance from a switch tender that the line was clear. In actuality the Alameda train, slightly behind schedule though still entitled to the right of way, had not yet come through. The two engines demolished each other. The number of casualties, though heavy, was not reported. (*Frank Leslie's Illustrated Newspaper*, December 11, 1869.)

The history of Western railroading intersected with the rise of the labor movement in the spring of 1886 as nationwide agitation for an "eight-hour day with no cut in pay" was at its height. A series of strikes across the country polarized attitudes on both sides. In this picture, members of an armed citizens' committee in Fort Worth, Texas, are arresting a "turbulent" striker after a violent demonstration on   April 3. A month later the anarchist bombing at Chicago's Haymarket Square marked a crucial turning point. The violence in Chicago cost organized labor the support of a large segment of the general public, and set back the cause of unionization in general. Only after the turn of the century would union membership in America reach the levels of pre-Haymarket days. (*Frank Leslie's Illustrated Newspaper*, April 17, 1886.)

A new mode of transportation led inevitably to a new mode of crime. Artist Edward Penfield titled this 1892 engraving "The Modern Dick Turpin" after the legendary eighteenth-century English highwayman. By the 1890s train robberies were a well-established fact of life in the American West. Jesse James and his gang had robbed their first train in Adair, Iowa, in July 1873, taking $3,000 from the safe of a Chicago, Rock Island & Pacific express delivery car. The James gang and its many counterparts quickly progressed from humble beginnings to bolder and much more lucrative exploits. (*Harper's Weekly*, January 16, 1892; Edward Penfield.)

Cowboys and Cattle

THE ANCESTORS OF THE Texas longhorn, the cattle that made the American cowboy, were brought to North America by the Spanish, beginning with Columbus' second voyage in 1493. Gradually, the cattle spread throughout Spanish territories in the New World. In Texas, in the first decades of the nineteenth century, these cattle from Spanish Mexico bred with cattle brought south by emigrants from the Northern states. In the 1840s, after Texas had won its war for independence from Mexico, more than 300,000 cattle were left running loose by Mexicans in southern Texas. These wild herds multiplied during the Civil War, when they were left largely untended. By the end of the war there were at least five million unbranded cattle between the Rio Grande and the Nueces Rivers. They were worth little in Texas, $3 to $4 a head, but they were there for the taking. If a way could be found to transport them to fill the growing demand for beef in the East, they would be worth ten times what they were worth in Texas. From these conditions of supply and demand the era of the great Texas cattle drives was born.

In 1866 some Texas ranchers decided to drive their herds northeast to the nearest railhead where they planned to sell them to Eastern buyers. Their destination was Sedalia, Missouri, and the Sedalia Trail, beginning in south Texas, became the first, though shortest-lived, of the major Texas cattle trails.

A quarter of a million longhorns were put on the Sedalia Trail in the spring and summer of 1866. For the cattlemen the plan quickly proved to be a terrible fiasco. The route across east Texas, a corner of the Indian Territory and parts of Arkansas and Missouri crossed swampy and heavily wooded land where the animals were hard to control and frequent stampedes left dead cattle scattered across the country. Worse, the cattle drivers met armed resistance from both Indians and settlers. Many farmers feared the Texas longhorns because they carried ticks that transmitted disease to other animals although the longhorns themselves were immune to their effects. Very few Texas cattle reached Sedalia in 1866. Some ranchers, as they learned of the problems they would face, diverted their herds to Baxter Springs, Kansas. There wasn't enough grass around Baxter Springs, however, to maintain all the cattle until buyers could be found, and many herds were abandoned to die of starvation.

Aware of the problems that Texas cattlemen were having on the Sedalia Trail in 1866, an Illinois cattle dealer named Joseph McCoy conceived the idea of establishing a cattle market for Texas ranchers at Abilene, Kansas, on the Kansas–Pacific Railroad, 150 miles west of Sedalia. To reach Abilene, cattle could be driven due north from the heart of the Texas cattle country around San Antonio, thereby avoiding the wooded land, farmers and Indians to the east. While McCoy built the necessary facilities at Abilene, a part-Cherokee trader named Jesse Chisholm scouted sections of the 600-mile trail north from San Antonio that came to bear his name. Despite a late start, 35,000 cattle reached Abilene on the Chisholm Trail in 1867. In the next four years a million and a half Texas longhorns rumbled into the Abilene stockyards in the first phase of the cattle-driving era that would see over five million head trailed north to Kansas by the early 1880s. The railroads were pushing farther west all the time, however, and as the 1870s wore on, new cattle trails were opened west of the Chisholm. New cattle towns such as Ellsworth and Dodge City, Kansas, and Ogalalla, Nebraska, came to supplant Abilene as centers of the cattle trade.

The first herds of cattle driven north were small, 500 to a few thousand head each. In a year or two, as the cattle drives developed, the herds were increased, and by the early 1870s several thousand head of cattle in a herd was commonplace. The largest herds ever driven north were about 15,000 strong. Cattle drives generally began in March or April so the animals would have spring grass to feed on along the way. Seven or eight cowboys, a trail boss who rode ahead to select camping sites and a cook driving a chuck wagon would have charge of each herd. The cattle were driven hard at first to tire them and lessen the chances of stampedes. Once they were trail broken, however, ten miles a day was considered a good pace as speed was not as important as arriving in Kansas with the herd intact and healthy. A successful drive was one on which the cattle gained weight, as they would be sold in Kansas by the pound. Location of water dictated much of the trail boss's strategy. Cattle on a drive would each drink up to 30 gallons of water every day, and cowboys dreaded a "dry drive" where there was little or no water to be found. Cattle on a dry drive eventually became crazed from thirst, and often tried to return on their own to the last place they had found water. Able to smell water ten miles off, the thirsty longhorns would then stampede wildly at the first scent of it.

The horses ridden by cowboys on the trail were supplied by the ranchers. For a long drive, each cowboy would need six or more horses, riding each one for several hours every other day. The remuda, or herd of saddle horses, would be driven along with the cattle under the supervision of a young cowboy called a wrangler. The more experienced cowboys rode at the front of the herd to try to catch stampedes early, and to keep the herd on the trail and prevent it from mixing with other herds. Other cowboys would space themselves out along the sides of the herd. Beginners got the unpopular drag-riding assignment of bringing up the rear, watching for strays and prodding the slower, footsore cattle that fell behind, all the while riding under a choking cloud of trail dust.

The mythic image of the American cowboy was born on the long drives. Reading the authentic memoirs that survive, it was clearly a way of life that many genuinely loved, but it was hardly as romantic as it was made out to be. The first thing to remember about the 40,000 or so men who worked as cowboys in the last half of the nineteenth century is that they were young. They had to be. On cattle drives, they rode for 18 to 20 hours a day for months, spent days without end in the broiling sun, slept in the rain—most cowboy deaths were from riding accidents or pneumonia—chased stampedes, prodded unruly steers across one muddy river after another, risked drowning while pulling mired cattle out of quicksand, fended off rattlesnakes, rustlers and Indians, and ate and drank little except stew, beans, biscuits, bacon and black coffee. It was a hard way, even in 1880, to earn $150 for a summer's work.

The classical era of the American cowboy, the era of the long drives, ended almost as quickly as it began. By the middle of the 1880s cattle were being raised on the northern plains in Colorado, Wyoming and Montana. The railroads themselves gradually pushed into the Texas cattle country, eliminating the need for long drives. At the same time, the invention of barbed wire, first patented in 1874, was gradually cutting off the open range. By the end of the 1880s Kansas was controlled by farmers and settlers who opposed the longhorns, which trampled their crops and infected their livestock. They finally declared the state off limits to Texas beef and backed up the prohibition with rifles. The cowboy didn't fade from history. Cowboys were still needed to tend the herds both in Texas and in the Northern states; the skills they perfected would be passed down from generation to generation, and are still practiced today.

OPPOSITE: A detail from a classic Remington illustration: a cowboy riding full bore across the prairie, fighting a prairie fire by pulling the hide of a freshly killed steer across the flames. This fire-fighting technique was learned from the Indians, who used buffalo hides the same way. (*Harper's Weekly*, October 27, 1888; Frederic Remington.)

OPPOSITE, TOP: Texas longhorns crossing a stream in east Texas or Louisiana in 1867, just as the era of the cattle drive was beginning. This was the first view of a cattle drive to appear in the nation's illustrated press. The term "cowboy" did not come into general use until the 1880s. *Harper's* referred to "stock-farmers" and "stock-drivers" in describing this picture. (*Harper's Weekly*, October 19, 1867; A. R. Waud.) OPPOSITE, BOTTOM: Cowboys guarding a herd on the open range at night. During much of the year, herds of cattle on Texas ranches would be allowed to graze unguarded. This was possible because ranches were widely scattered, and cattle would not normally wander too far from water holes. Prior to going up the trail to Kansas, however, the herds would be guarded each night to keep them together. Once on the trail, guards were absolutely necessary, one of the reasons why cowboys got so little sleep. When a herd had been settled peacefully, two men on horseback could guard several thousand cattle by circling them in opposite directions. Cowboys often sang to the cattle at night to keep them calm. So many cowboy songs are slow and sentimental ballads because those were the songs the cattle preferred. Spending so much time guarding cattle at night, cowboys learned to use the night sky as compass and watch. On the trail the cook would point the tongue of his chuck wagon at the North Star before going to sleep. This would tell the cowboys in which direction to drive the herd the following morning. Cowboys on night duty could time the length of their shifts by following the rotation of the Big Dipper. On cloudy nights, however, many found they could rely on their horses to tell them when their shifts

were over. Experienced cow ponies would often head back to camp on their own after exactly two hours with the herd. (*Harper's Weekly*, March 28, 1874; Frenzeny and Tavernier.) ABOVE: Texas cowboys trying to stop a stampede of cattle frightened by thunder and lightning near Kerrville, 70 miles northeast of San Antonio, in 1881. Thunder and lightning were probably the most common cause of stampedes, though any sudden noise, even the rattling of a coffee cup or the striking of a match, could set one off, and some began for no discernible reason. Each herd developed its own personality; some stampeded often, others never. Occasionally cowboys would discover a ringleader among the steers that seemed always ready to lead a stampede. They often found that sewing the steer's eyelids together could change this tendency. During the two or three weeks it took for the threads to rot through so the animal could see again, it generally became much more peaceful. To stop a stampede it was necessary to turn the head cattle, and force them to run in an increasingly tight circle where they would eventually tire, mill around and stop. Cowboys would push their very game horses to the front of the herds, and, if all else failed, fire their guns across the leaders' faces. Still, some stampedes went on for hours, leaving cattle lost, scattered and often dead, trampled by faster, wilder steers. The cowboys faced hours or even days of rounding up the herd and getting it back on the trail. The worst recorded stampede of this era left 2,000 cattle dead on the range. (*Frank Leslie's Illustrated Newspaper*, May 28, 1881; L. W. Macdonald.)

ABOVE: *Harper's* artists Paul Frenzeny and Jules Tavernier never went on a cattle drive, but they did accompany a group of Texas ranchers and cattlemen on a deer hunt, illustrated here, in the area around Denison in the early 1870s. Kept up late into the night as stories were told around the campfire, they felt the attraction of a life on the range. (*Harper's Weekly*, February 28, 1874; Frenzeny and Tavernier.) OPPOSITE, TOP: Texas cattle being driven into Dodge City, Kansas, in 1878 when Dodge was at its peak as the cattle capital of the West. The Santa Fe Railroad reached Dodge in 1872, and Dodge quickly became the center for shipping both cattle and buffalo hides to the East. By 1876 many herds from the area around Bandera, Texas, were following the new Western Trail to Dodge. Dodge was the wildest, roughest and longest-lived of the Kansas cattle towns, and herds continued to pour in every summer for another decade. (*Frank Leslie's Illustrated Newspaper*, July 27, 1878; Edward Rapier.) OPPOSITE, BOTTOM: Longhorns being herded into a cattle chute at Abilene from which they would be loaded aboard railroad cars for shipment East. This picture was drawn in 1871 at the height of Abilene's prosperity. Abilene was the first Kansas cattle town, a wild oasis at the end of the trail where trail bosses could close the sale of a herd worth tens of thousands of dollars with a handshake over a drink with an Eastern buyer at one of the many saloons. The ordinary cowboys, after months of long days in the saddle, got paid off and spent their wages on haircuts, new clothes, whiskey, poker and prostitutes before heading back to Texas. Abilene was rough, but not quite as rough as legend would have it. In eight months as Abilene's sheriff in 1871, James Butler (Wild Bill) Hickok only shot and killed two men, one of them, a fellow peace officer, by accident. In five Kansas cattle towns combined—Abilene, Ellsworth, Dodge, Wichita and Caldwell—there were only 45 documented homicides between 1870 and 1885, and many of these were unrelated to the cattle trade. (*Frank Leslie's Illustrated Newspaper*, August 19, 1871; Albert Berghaus, from a sketch by Henry Worrall.)

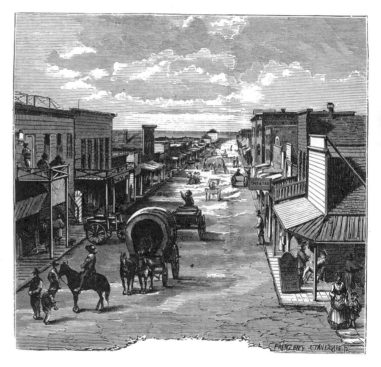

Four scenes from the *Harper's* series on the Texas cattle industry in which the term "cowboy" was finally used. TOP, LEFT: Branding cattle before the start of the drive north. Cattle were driven into a narrow path between two wooden fences, and the hot branding irons applied. Every ranch had its own brand, made up of the initials of the ranch's name or some other distinctive mark. TOP,

RIGHT: A little trading post on the Ninnescah River, one of the few signs of civilization the cowboys would pass on the drive north to Kansas. BOTTOM, LEFT: Loading the cattle on a train in Kansas for shipment to Eastern markets. BOTTOM, RIGHT: Wichita, Kansas, in the early 1870s, during its period as a thriving cow town. (*Harper's Weekly*, May 2, 1874; Frenzeny and Tavernier.)

ABOVE: The end of the trail, Texas cattle in a Kansas corral. When Joseph McCoy conceived the idea of setting up a market for Texas cattle in Abilene, the scheme was widely ridiculed as impractical. For $2,400 McCoy was able to buy 480 acres in Abilene. He built a hotel for the cattlemen he knew would come and stockyards for the cattle. The Kansas–Pacific Railroad didn't believe in the idea either. The Railroad gave McCoy a contract calling for him to receive one-eighth of the freight charged for shipping cattle out of Abilene. After a year or two it owed him so much money that it repudiated the contract, and he only collected years later after extensive litigation. His 1874 book, *Historic Sketches of the Cattle Trade*, is one of the basic sources of information on the cattle-driving era. (*Harper's Weekly*, April 28, 1888; Frederic Remington.) OVERLEAF: Cowboys fighting a prairie fire. Such fires were common in dry areas where they could be started easily by lightning, by a carelessly thrown match or by Indians. The first thing to do in the face of an approaching prairie fire was to plow a wide furrow, as the men at left are doing, to create a firebreak. Meanwhile, a backfire would be started and diverted toward the approaching flames along kerosene-drenched ropes. The two fires going in opposite directions would check each other if the wind was not too strong. Cowboys would guard the downwind side of the firebreak to extinguish sparks with water and blankets. (*Frank Leslie's Illustrated Newspaper*, July 17, 1886.)

ABOVE: A band of Texas cowboys shooting up the main street of a small Southwestern town. To prevent scenes like this, many cow towns required cowboys coming in from a cattle drive to check their guns with the sheriff on arrival. To his law-abiding neighbors, farmers and tradesmen, and, above all, to the Eastern press, the exploits of the American cowboy when blowing off steam fed the myth that he was the personification of Western wildness. This is one of the earliest published illustrations on a theme later developed by Zogbaum, Remington, Charles M. Russell and many other Western artists. (*Frank Leslie's Illustrated Newspaper*, January 14, 1882; Paul Frenzeny.) LEFT: Cowboys playfully terrorizing passengers on a Southern Pacific train in the mid-1880s. According to the *Frank Leslie's* correspondent, the cowboys forced whiskey on their fellow passengers and then ordered them to buy the pecans usually sold by boys on Western trains, all the while keeping up a steady stream of gunfire that fortunately left no one injured. It is safe to say that when cowboys let off steam this way they were often just living up to their press notices and their dime-novel image, of which by the 1880s they were well aware. (*Frank Leslie's Illustrated Newspaper*, January 17, 1885; A. F. Blauvelt.)

A raid on a Texas cattle ranch by rustlers from across the border in Mexico as drawn by W. M. Cary for *Harper's* in 1874. As there is no record that the artist, who had spent time on the northern plains, ever visited Texas, this probably represents a scene imagined from published accounts of cattle rustling, a subject very often in the news as the cattle industry developed. Cattle rustlers developed their craft into a fine art as the century wore on. Methods were found of changing brands in such a way that even an experienced eye would have difficulty detecting the difference. In some areas mere possession of a running iron, a piece of metal with a curved end used to alter brands, was enough to qualify its owner for immediate hanging by vigilantes. Rustlers who didn't want to risk brand changing learned ways to lead desirable unbranded calves away from their mothers. One way was to cut the muscles that controlled their eyelids. Unable to find their mothers, the calves would go wherever the rustlers wanted to drive them. These methods worked because Texas ranches were often so big that guarding them was impossible. By the 1880s, for example, the XIT Ranch along the New Mexico border was spread over three million acres on which 150,000 head of cattle were herded, and 35,000 calves branded, every year. (*Harper's Weekly,* January 31, 1874; W. M. Cary.)

ABOVE: A flock of Texas sheep being driven away from a prairie fire. Throughout the nineteenth century, Western cattlemen considered sheep and sheepherders to be their natural enemies. The cattlemen resented the intrusion of sheep ranchers on the open range. They believed that sheep destroyed grazing land for cattle by eating the grass too close to the roots, which were then cut by the sheep's sharp hooves. Working cowboys, who were famous for never walking ten yards if they could ride, were known to refuse to associate with sheepherders, who often worked on foot. (*Frank Leslie's Illustrated Newspaper*, October 28, 1882.) OPPO-SITE, TOP: During the winter of 1881–82 an envelope arrived at the New York offices of *Harper's Weekly* containing a single crude sketch drawn on plain wrapping paper of several cowboys being roused from sleep by a mounted scout warning them of impending danger. The sketch was turned over to *Harper's* staff artist W. A. Rogers, who redrew it directly on the woodblock for publication. The result was the first appearance in print of any work by Frederic Remington, who went on from this beginning to become the greatest Western illustrator that the nineteenth century produced. Remington, then 19 years old, had spent several weeks in the fall of 1881 in Montana, where he was introduced to the cowboy life, to which he would return often in illustrations, paintings and sculptures during the rest of his prolific career. In

keeping with the casual journalistic practices of the day, *Harper's* used this sketch to illustrate an article dealing with cattle rustling in the vicinity of Tombstone, Arizona, despite the fact that neither Remington nor Rogers had ever set foot in that territory. It should be seen as a picture of cowboy life on the northern plains. (*Harper's Weekly*, February 25, 1882; W. A. Rogers, from a sketch by Frederic Remington.) OPPOSITE, BOTTOM: A Remington illustration of a quarrel over a card game on a New Mexico ranch. New Mexico became prominent in the cattle industry in the same post–Civil War years that saw the first trail drives to Kansas. Just after the war ended, Texas ranchers Charles Goodnight and Oliver Loving decided to drive cattle north to sell to miners in the Colorado mining camps. To avoid the Comanches and the Kiowas, they trailed their herd west from central Texas, and then followed the Pecos River north through New Mexico to Colorado. Others followed their example, and by 1869 more than a million head had been trailed north on what came to be called the Goodnight–Loving Trail. Only a portion of these cattle were sold to miners. The rest were used to establish the first cattle ranches in New Mexico and on the northern plains, where millions of acres of free public-domain grassland were waiting to be used. (*Harper's Weekly*, April 23, 1887; Frederic Remington.)

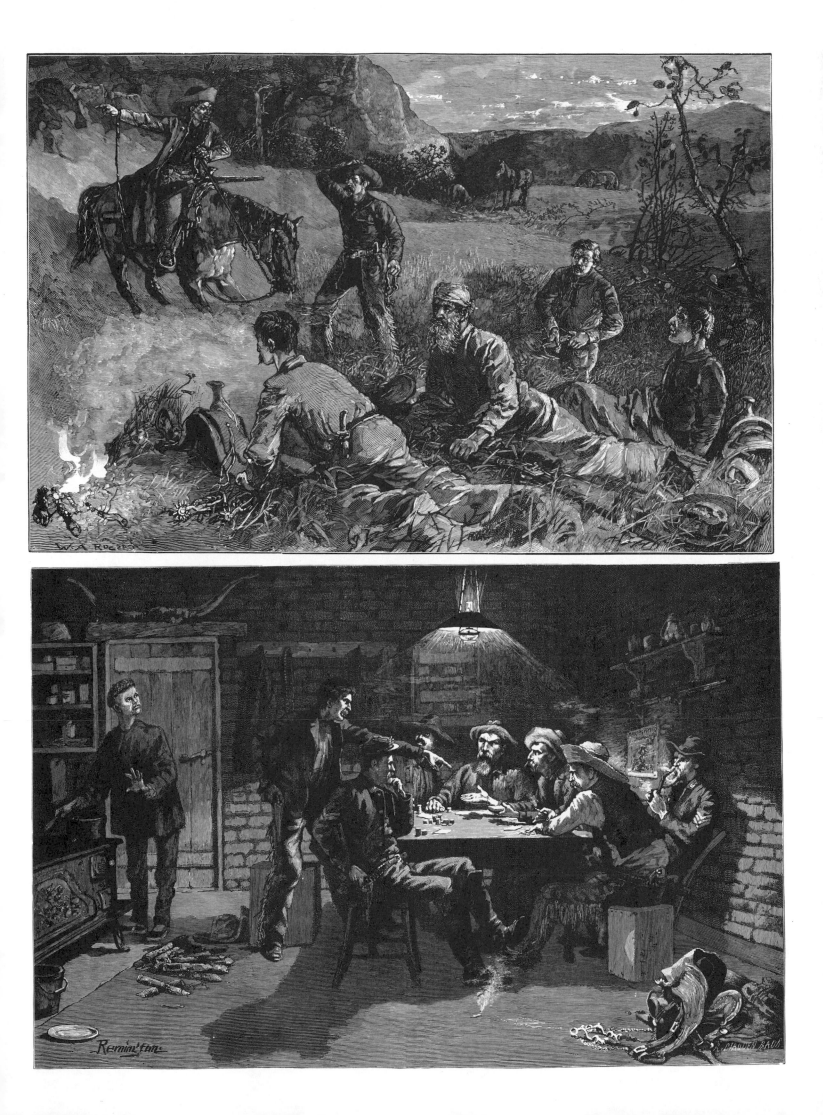

ABOVE: Branding a mustang in a California corral. California had a cattle-ranching industry from the earliest decades of the nineteenth century, though the Spanish–Mexican ranches declined somewhat after California was ceded to the United States in 1848 and overrun by the Gold Rush a year later. Unlike the Texas cowboy, the Mexican vaquero of the great California ranches never captured the popular imagination of nineteenth-century America, though his skills with livestock were just as great. Cattle were even trailed long distances in California years before the idea took hold in Texas, but the California cattle drives didn't produce any authors like Charlie Siringo, Andy Adams and Teddy Blue Abbott, men who lived the Texas–Kansas cattle drives and then told their stories to an eager public. (*Frank Leslie's Illustrated Newspaper*, March 14, 1874; A. Lemon.) OPPOSITE, TOP: Cowboys in Colorado doing a part of every cowboy's work, roping and branding calves. *Harper's* artist W. A. Rogers took a trip West in 1879 that produced a series of illustrations on the cowboys and ranches of Colorado. By the end of the 1870s cattle ranching was a major industry in the Colorado–Wyoming area. Colorado cattle baron John Wesley Iliff had come West to search for gold during the 1859 Pike's Peak Gold Rush. Iliff didn't find much gold, but he saw the potential for cattle on the northern plains and stayed to build a prosperous ranch in northeast Colorado. Others followed his example. Rogers wrote in 1879 that the largest Colorado herds—some up to 40,000 head—were worth more than many Rocky Mountain gold and silver mines. These northern herds were all started with longhorns imported from Texas. By the 1880s, however, especially on the northern plains but in Texas as well, the pure longhorn was fast being replaced by new breeds created by the introduction of other varieties of cattle—shorthorn, Hereford and Aberdeen Angus. The hardy longhorn had been the perfect animal to endure the rigors of the long cattle drives, but the meat it produced tended to be lean and tough. Another disadvantage was that the longhorn didn't reach its mature weight of about 1,200 pounds until it was ten years old. When the trail-driving era ended in the 1880s, ranchers switched quickly to more productive and profitable varieties of cattle. Today the Texas longhorn may be seen only in the movies. (*Harper's Weekly*, October 6, 1883; W. A. Rogers.)

RIGHT: The central figure from a classic Remington illustration, "In from the Night Herd." A cowboy returns to camp from his shift of guard duty. A cowboy would use his best horse for night duty, and would soon find out which of his other horses were best at swimming rivers while mounted, or pulling bogged-down cattle out of quicksand. Cowboys usually carried rifles only in particularly dangerous country as they were uncomfortable for both horse and rider on a long drive. (*Harper's Weekly*, October 9, 1886; Frederic Remington.)

Preparing supper at roundup time on the northern plains. In Texas, ranches were widely scattered, and cattle from one ranch seldom mixed with those from another. At Texas roundups, held in the spring, new calves were branded, and the cattle to be put on the trail and sold that year were selected. In the fall roundup, animals missed in the spring would be branded. On the northern plains, herds from many ranches grazed together on common grassland much of the year. In those areas, cooperative roundups were held twice a year. In the spring, ranchers would pool their cowboys and horses to bring in the herds, which had been untended throughout the winter, in order to sort and brand new calves. As calves would always stay with their mothers, it was easy to tell which brand to give them. At the fall roundup, mature cattle to be sold after a summer's grazing would be selected. Charles Goodnight invented the chuck wagon in 1866 when he nailed a cupboard on the back of an ordinary ranch wagon. Chuck wagons carried food, medicine, ammunition, bedrolls, spare saddles and other equipment. On cattle drives, the cook drove the chuck wagon ahead of the herd to have supper ready when the day's drive was over. At night on cattle drives or at roundup time, the chuck wagon served as the cowboys' headquarters. In today's era of ranching with trucks and helicopters, the chuck wagon is just about as extinct as the Texas longhorn. (*Frank Leslie's Illustrated Newspaper*, November 3, 1888; based on a photograph by C. D. Kirkland.)

One diversion of cowboy life, riding a bucking steer at roundup time. From cowboy pastimes such as this the modern rodeo developed. The illustrations on this and the preceding page were based on photographs by C. D. Kirkland of Cheyenne, Wyoming, a pioneer photographer and chronicler of the American cowboy on the northern plains. (*Frank Leslie's Illustrated Newspaper*, May 5, 1888; based on a photograph by C. D. Kirkland.)

ABOVE: *Illustrated London News* staff artist R. Caton Woodville traveled through the Western states and Canada in 1890 and 1891. He produced several hunting illustrations as well as an on-the-spot record of some of the events surrounding the Wounded Knee Massacre. This picture of a fall roundup in Wyoming's Big Horn country shows Indian horsemen driving cattle into a corral from where they will go to the nearest Northern Pacific station for shipment to Chicago's stockyards. (*The Illustrated London News*, October 3, 1891; R. Caton Woodville.) OPPOSITE: Two Remington illustrations from Theodore Roose-velt's *Ranch Life and the Hunting-Trail*, one of the basic books on ranching life on the northern plains in the last decades of the nineteenth century. Before entering politics, Roosevelt spent a great deal of time ranching in the Dakotas and came to know the animals, the land and the Western characters who lived on it very well. ABOVE: A cowboy cutting a steer out of the herd. Horses used for this task learned to anticipate the steer's every move. BELOW: A cowboy in a stampede, struggling to get in position to turn the lead steer. (Theodore Roosevelt: *Ranch Life and the Hunting-Trail*, 1888; Frederic Remington.)

ABOVE: Breaking wild horses was not usually a job for the average cowboy. Generally this task was entrusted to itinerant specialists who toured the ranches breaking mustangs for $5 a head. A good horseman could break several in a week, working with each horse each day until it was tame enough to be turned over to the ranch's regular cowboys. Mustangs were captured on the open range and brought in for breaking when they were about four years old. These illustrations were the result of a collaboration between two artists, Jerome H. Smith and Charles M. Russell. Russell was a working cowboy in Montana in the 1880s who went on after the turn of the century to become with Remington and Charles Schreyvogel one of the three best painters in the genre of cowboy art. This series of illustrations was one of the young Russell's first appearances in print. (*Frank Leslie's Illustrated Newspaper*, May 18, 1889; Jerome H. Smith and Charles M. Russell.) OPPOSITE, TOP: Cattle in a blizzard on the northern plains. By 1880 there were four and a half million cattle on the northern plains. Vast fortunes were being made by ranchers with sufficient capital to establish large herds, and many ranchers were protecting their investments by illegally fencing off huge tracts of public-domain grassland with barbed wire. In the winter of 1886–87, however, disaster struck. Later, old-timers would say they had known something was up because the muskrats' coats were fuller and longer than usual and the ducks and geese flew south a month early. From Missouri to the Sierra, and from Canada to New Mexico, the heaviest snows in history combined with temperatures as low as 70 degrees below zero to devastate the cattle industry. In the bitter winter of 1886–87 ranchers on the northern plains learned the painful lesson that if it gets cold enough, most cattle, even when starving to death, cannot or will not paw through snow to find grass to eat, and also lack the horse's instinct to satisfy thirst by eating snow. Estimates vary, but anywhere from 50% to 90% of the cattle on the northern plains starved or froze to death that winter. As cattlemen panicked and sold off the animals they had left, the bottom fell out of the cattle market. Many ranchers went bankrupt, and many changes were quickly made in the ranching business. Ranchers now knew that their cattle could not be certain to survive winters on their own, so they dug wells for water and grew hay for food. They bought land, fenced it legally and cut the size of their herds to manageable proportions. Knowing they would have to be more businesslike to survive, they intensified breeding efforts, concentrating on the cattle that produced the most beef, the greatest yield per dollar. As the last of the long drives marked the end of an era for the ranchers of Texas, the blizzards of 1887 marked the end of an era, and the beginning of a new one, for the ranchers in the North. (*Harper's Weekly*, February 27, 1886; Charles Graham, from a sketch by Henry Worrall.) OPPOSITE, BOTTOM: Remington's original title for this picture was "Thanksgiving Dinner for the Ranch." (*Harper's Weekly*, November 24, 1888; Frederic Remington.) OVERLEAF: Four cowboys charging down the main street of a little town as soldiers, Indians, Chinese laborers, prospectors and townsmen watch in awe, fear and amazement. Originally titled "Painting the Town Red," Zogbaum's picture was used to illustrate an article on cowboys by a writer named G. O. Shields. Shields attempted to convince *Harper's* readers that cowboys were kind, friendly, warm-spirited fellows who occasionally let their innocent fun get a little out of hand. This was basically true, but it wasn't convincing. Thousands of cowboys worked at their jobs for years and never saw a gun fired for any purpose more violent than shooting a wild turkey, killing a rattlesnake or putting an injured animal out of its misery. In the East, however, the image of the cowboy was defined by the reckless violence and lawlessness portrayed in the *Police Gazette* and the dime novels of the period. (*Harper's Weekly*, October 16, 1886; R. F. Zogbaum.)

LEFT: A fight in a cattle-town saloon erupts into gunfire at close range. (Theodore Roosevelt: *Ranch Life and the Hunting-Trail*, 1888; Frederic Remington.) BELOW: Cattlemen and Indians in conflict over the land. Like the pioneer of the wagon-train era, like the buffalo hunter, the prospector, the settler and the railroad builder, the cattle rancher also sometimes moved onto the Indians' traditional lands, and, like those before him, sometimes had to fight for it. (Theodore Roosevelt: *Ranch Life and the Hunting-Trail*, 1888; Frederic Remington.) OPPOSITE: The vast loneliness of the northern plains surrounds this solitary cowboy stopping to mail a letter at a prairie mailbox made from an old dried-beef container. (*Harper's Weekly*, April 23, 1887; R. F. Zogbaum.)

ABOVE: A cowboy, broke and out of work for the winter, auctioning off his horse on the main street of a northern frontier town in the 1880s. For an average horse in decent condition, with saddle and other equipment included, the cowboy after a good deal of effort might have been paid about $40 in a region where horses were plentiful and money was scarce. Horses were traded freely among Western cowboys, but a man had to be desperate for funds to throw in his saddle and other equipment. Among cowboys, the expression "sold his saddle" was a euphemism for retiring from the cowboy trade for good. (*Harper's Weekly*, December 24, 1887; R.

F. Zogbaum.) OPPOSITE, TOP: Colorado cowboys living in a dugout through a long northern winter. Winter was a dull time for cowboys, who even if they had jobs had to devise ways, such as the never-ending poker game, of passing the time. On some big ranches, cowboys might spend lonely winter months as line riders stationed at outpost camps far from the ranch's main head-quarters. Their job would be to patrol the range for rustlers, keep an eye on the barbed-wire fences if the range was fenced or try to keep the cattle from straying too far if it wasn't. (*Harper's Weekly*, November 18, 1882; W. A. Rogers.)

LEFT: A cowboy of the 1880s. The broad-brimmed cowboy hat not only protected the wearer from the blazing sun, but could serve as a pillow or a drinking cup, for man or horse, when needed. (*Frank Leslie's Illustrated Newspaper*, April 9, 1887; based on a photograph by C. D. Kirkland.)

Army Life

AT FIRST GLANCE it would seem that the United States Army faced a hopeless task in the West in the years after the end of the Civil War. The Union Army had about a million soldiers in uniform when the Confederacy surrendered in 1865. A war-weary Congress, representing an equally war-weary nation, quickly slashed the military budget, reducing the size of the Army by statute to 54,000 men in 1866, and reducing it again, to 27,000 men, in 1874. At any given time only a fraction of even these reduced numbers served in the West. In an area of two and a half million square miles, this minuscule force of soldiers was strung out in almost 100 forts and outposts between the Mississippi River and the Pacific Ocean. Companies were isolated from each other, with communication—depending mostly on mounted couriers—slow and difficult. Somehow, fewer than 10,000 poorly equipped, poorly trained, badly fed, often ineptly led, underpaid soldiers had to contend with perhaps 300,000 Indians of whom about half might be considered hostile.

The soldiers' tasks were to defend settlers, miners, ranchers and railroad builders, to survey new routes and above all to deter Indian raids at a time when incursions onto the Indians' traditional lands were growing almost daily in number and intensity and were arousing continually higher levels of resentment, opposition and violence. Yet despite the pitfalls, the problems and the obstacles, the Indian Wars were concluded only 25 years after the Civil War. The end of armed resistance to the expansion of the white man's frontier was made manifest by the final surrender of Geronimo and his followers in Arizona in 1886, and the historic Wounded Knee Massacre on South Dakota's Pine Ridge Reservation at the end of 1890.

To fight the Indians the Army had to learn new ways of doing its job. It learned that to support troops of soldiers with wagon trains of supplies made it impossible to follow Indians into rough terrain. In the 1870s Gen. George Crook substituted pack mules for the wagons where necessary. The Army discovered that the Indians had an immense disadvantage in that they were defending their homelands where their families, wives, children and defenseless elders also lived. This made them vulnerable to all-out attacks that ignored the rules of civilized warfare and treated everyone in a given area as a target. The Army also learned that even the most warlike tribes of Plains Indians traditionally never fought in the winter. Thus the soldiers often resorted to surprise attacks on the winter camps where the Indians lived with their families. Moreover, the Indians, despite their numerical advantages, were fragmented in many ways, and coalitions among them were unsteady. The Army played on ancient animosities and turned tribe against tribe, and even Indian against Indian. Though many Indians were, individually, fearsome warriors, the Army didn't fight them individually. Even with its numerical restrictions, the Army generally had the manpower to build up its forces in any given area to the point where it could eventually win control.

There were few to argue about the morality of any of this, to suggest that there might be another way, or that the Indians of North America represented ancient cultures whose customs, accomplishments and ways of life were deserving of respect from the white man. All too often the military was turned loose under the leadership of fanatics. Given the attitudes of white America in the nineteenth century, there is a feeling of inevitability about the outcome of the Indian Wars. Between 1860 and 1890 the Indian Wars were won with the expenditure of such a meager portion of the nation's resources that it is impossible to conceive, with the ever-increasing pressure of westward expansion, that the outcome could ever have been any different.

For soldiers who came of age during the great campaigns of the Civil War, the experience of soldiering in the West during the Indian Wars must have come initially as a shock. Some Western forts were so small during the Indian Wars that they were manned by a single company of 30 to 40 men. When at peace, there was absolutely nothing to do at these outposts, and accounts of extreme boredom are common. The larger forts, often built at crucial junctions on important trails, gave the soldiers who manned them at least the diversion presented by the comings and goings of an active frontier center. Whether at large forts or small frontier outposts, the details of Army life on the Western frontier were much the same. It was hardly glamorous. The food was notoriously poor: stew, beans, hardtack, salt pork, potatoes, dried apples and coffee. Fresh vegetables were rare except in areas settled enough for the soldiers to plant small gardens themselves, and scurvy haunted the forts as it did the mining camps. Sleeping quarters, especially for the lower ranks, were primitive and crowded. Sanitation was poor, and water often polluted. As with the pioneers on the wagon trains, many more soldiers died in the nineteenth century of cholera or smallpox than were killed by the Indians. Uniforms were made of wool that was much too hot in the summer, and still let soldiers freeze in the winter. The pay, which arrived once every two months under the best of conditions, was not enticing: $13 a month for privates in the 1870s, $15 for corporals and $22 for first sergeants. Professional gamblers, whiskey peddlers and prostitutes followed the Army throughout the West, as they followed the miners and the railroad builders, ready to relieve even a private of his salary.

The small Army of the period of the Indian Wars was dominated by a few striking personalities, all of whom will always be overshadowed by the aura that still attaches itself to the Custer legend. Charming, vain, vindictive, decisive, a student of strategy who spent most of his spare time in his last years writing his memoirs, Custer almost missed his date with Sitting Bull, Crazy Horse and Gall on the Little Bighorn. Testifying before a Congressional committee in March 1876 concerning fraud in the Indian service, Custer so irritated President Grant that the President removed him from his command and ordered his nonparticipation in the forthcoming expedition against the Sioux and their allies. A wave of popular and political protest, and the entreaties of Gen. Alfred Terry, who needed him, got Custer back his regiment.

In the career of one soldier, Gen. Nelson A. Miles, one can almost follow the whole history of the Indian Wars. After lengthy service in the Civil War, Miles took command of the Fifth Infantry. In the mid-1870s he defeated the Cheyenne, Kiowa and Comanche on the Staked Plains of west Texas, and in the aftermath of Little Bighorn chased Sitting Bull across the border to Canada and fought against Crazy Horse and other chiefs on the northern plains. In 1877 he captured the Nez Percé under Chief Joseph and the following year neutralized Elk Horn's Bannock Indians near Yellowstone Park. In the 1880s Miles commanded the final victory over Geronimo in Arizona, and at the end of the decade suppressed the potentially serious Sioux uprising at the time of Wounded Knee. If he had been involved in more popular wars, Miles would surely be remembered as one of the most remarkable soldiers in American history. He died in 1925 at the age of 85.

OPPOSITE: One of the hazards of Army duty in the Southwest: an ambushed guard is dragged off across the desert by his frightened horse. (*Harper's Weekly*, June 8, 1889; Frederic Remington.)

OPPOSITE, TOP: The flag of the state of Texas, which had been admitted to the Union in 1845, flying above the Alamo in San Antonio in March 1861, just a month before the start of the Civil War. On March 6, 1836, the Alamo, an old Spanish Franciscan mission, had been the scene of the famous defeat suffered by a small force fighting for Texas' independence at the hands of a Mexican army led by Gen. Antonio de Santa Anna. All 188 defenders of the Alamo were killed, including legendary frontiersman Davy Crockett and Col. Jim Bowie. The victory of the Mexicans was short-lived. The following month, on April 21, the Texas Army under Gen. Sam Houston surprised Santa Anna at the San Jacinto River near Galveston Bay, forced the Mexicans to surrender and secured the independence of Texas. (*Harper's Weekly*, March 23, 1861.) OPPOSITE, BOTTOM: Fort Snelling, Minnesota, one of the oldest U.S. Army installations in the West, built on an elevated bluff at the junction of the Minnesota and Mississippi Rivers. Zebulon Pike had camped near this spot during his travels in the early years of the century, and the Army had first established a base there in 1819. Construction on the fort seen here began in 1840. In the early days it was an isolated camp, and supplies were often slow to arrive. It is recorded that in the winter

of 1820–21 the camp's quartermaster, having run out of paper, sent his accounts to Washington on strips of birch bark. In 1823 an early stern-wheel steamboat, the *Virginia*, ascended the Mississippi to Fort Snelling. The coming of steam to the upper Mississippi made life easier. Troops and supplies could now reach the camp from St. Louis in about a week. Previously, traveling by keelboat, 60 days had been considered making good time. (*Ballou's Pictorial Drawing-Room Companion*, n.d.) ABOVE: Fort Bridger, on Black's Fork of the Green River in the southeastern part of present-day Wyoming. Established as a trading post by the legendary mountain man Jim Bridger in the early 1840s, the fort was a resting place for many wagon trains on the Oregon Trail. It was located about 100 miles southeast of the South Pass through the Rockies. A visit to the fort lengthened the trip to Oregon or California by a week or more, but did provide the opportunity to repair wagons and purchase essential supplies before the difficult mountain crossings that lay ahead. When this view was drawn in 1858, the fort was occupied by two U.S. Army companies who lived through bitterly cold winters in the primitive tents pictured here. (*Frank Leslie's Illustrated Newspaper*, July 10, 1858.)

OPPOSITE, TOP: Soldiers in the U.S. Cavalry during mounted pistol practice in 1889. Practice in this difficult skill was needed by the horses as well as by the soldiers. (*Harper's Weekly*, January 12, 1889; R. F. Zogbaum.) OPPOSITE, BOTTOM: A supply train of Army wagons pulled by teams of mules crossing a Western stream. On the right a contingent of soldiers is helping pull a loaded wagon up the steep incline to the top of the ravine. The mounted soldiers are stationed in the water to mark the line of the crossing for the wagon drivers, and to rescue any mules swept off their feet by the current. Cavalry troops on the march were followed by well-guarded supply trains such as this bringing food, ammunition and camp equipment. The wagons were usually driven by civilian wagon drivers or "mule-whackers," one of the more colorful classes of Western characters. It was common to encounter rivers and streams where the muddy bottom was so slippery that fully loaded wagons couldn't get across. On those occasions, wagons would be half unloaded, led across, the remaining cargo unpacked, led back across and repacked, etc. It could often take a day or two for a typical column to make such a river crossing. (*Harper's Weekly*, November 16, 1889; R. F. Zogbaum.) ABOVE: *Harper's* published this sketch by its military specialist, R. F. Zogbaum, under the title "Cavalry on the March—Danger Ahead." It was standard practice to have advance guards and flankers in hostile territory. These troopers would check anything—a ravine, group of trees or large rock—big enough to conceal the enemy. Cavalry troops could ordinarily move at the rate of 20 to 25 miles a day, the exact distance determined by the

location of good camping sites with grass and water for the horses. Troops started between six and seven in the morning, earlier in hot climates, and stopped about once an hour, dismounting so the horses could rest. The typical pace was a fast walk unless there was a reason to go faster. Under extreme necessity, the Cavalry could do unusual things. It was reported that in the Ute campaign of 1879, a Fifth Cavalry column covered 170 miles in just over three days without losing a horse, and was ready to go into action on arrival. (*Harper's Weekly*, September 28, 1889; R. F. Zogbaum.) OVERLEAF: Cavalry troops in the West were armed with both rifles and pistols. It required skill and effort to learn to shoot effectively with rifles while on horseback, either holding the reins while using both hands to aim and fire, or dropping the reins and controlling the well-schooled Cavalry horses without them. Indians were cunning fighters who seldom allowed themselves to be caught in pitched battles unless they had overwhelmingly superior numbers, or some other advantage. A great deal of the Indian fighting was done on foot, tracking down small groups or individuals in rugged terrain. At such times, dismounted troopers would lead their horses while carrying their carbines in a ready position. By the end of the Indian Wars it had become standard procedure for Cavalry troops on the march to be led by a line of advance scouts and troopers, such as those illustrated here, skilled in firing while mounted. Their job, where conditions called for it, was to clear a path for the main column by dislodging the enemy with mounted rifle fire. (*Harper's Weekly*, March 29, 1890; R. F. Zogbaum.)

R. F. Zogbaum

OPPOSITE, TOP: A Cavalry troop preparing for action in 1888. With swords, rifles and pistols, officers went into battle heavily armed, but it did take some time to get all of this equipment, and the horses, ready and mounted. (*Harper's Weekly*, 1888; R. F. Zogbaum.) OPPOSITE, BOTTOM: A moment of relaxation for soldiers in the West. The heavy coats worn inside the tents identify this as a winter scene. (*Harper's Weekly*, May 13, 1871; Julian Scott.) ABOVE: The arrival of the mail. Soldiers sit around their camp fires, with tents and supply wagons in the background, enjoying an event that occurred only once every several weeks, or even months. The fires, visible for miles across the prairie, would not have been lit if there were any danger of Indian attack. Indians often preferred to attack Army camps at dawn, having located them the evening before by their fires. Knowing this, when Indian attack was feared, Cavalry troops sometimes arrived at a camp in the late afternoon, lit their fires, cooked their dinner and then, under cover of darkness, moved to a new camp several miles away. The best location for any camp was just over the crest of a hill so that it would have to be approached from below. (*Harper's Weekly*, October 5, 1889; R. F. Zogbaum.)

OPPOSITE: When a Cavalry troop on the march camped for the night, small groups of soldiers like the one illustrated here would be stationed to guard any approach to the main camp. Picket duty made for a dangerous and nerve-racking night for the soldiers who tried to remain alert for any sound that might mean a surprise attack or ambush. As the sun rises over the plains, the soldiers at this outlying post are scanning the eastern horizon for a column of smoke, the telltale sign of an Indian village. As they climb the rocks to get a better view, weapons are kept out of sight—to prevent their being detected by the reflection of sunlight off a rifle barrel. (*Harper's Weekly*, August 3, 1889; R. F. Zogbaum.) ABOVE: An Army scout scanning the plains as the troops behind him prepare for the day's march. The Army would have been helpless in the West without the scouts attached to each command. They were civilians, often hunters or trappers who had lived their whole lives on the frontier. They knew how to survive in the wilderness, to ride without being seen, to travel at night if

needed to deliver information without getting lost, to follow a trail and to scent danger from signs invisible to others. The great scouts could read an epic in a hoofprint or a blade of grass. Were the animals being followed horses, mules or burros? If shod, to whom did they belong? Were they being ridden? Were they tired or fresh? How fast were they going? How many were there? How long ago had the trail been left? The answers to all of these questions were plain for the scouts to read along the trail. How a blade of grass was bitten off where a horse had stopped to graze could tell a scout whether or not it had a bit in its mouth. The type of trail left by cattle could help a scout lead his command to water—range cattle tend to stay in a clearly defined trail and go single file on their way to water; coming away from water they scatter to graze. Survival in the West, and victory in the Indian Wars, depended for the Cavalry on the knowledge and acumen of their scouts. (*Harper's Weekly*, August 11, 1888; R. F. Zogbaum.)

ABOVE: A Cavalry troop caught in a blizzard. Winter storms could come up suddenly on the frontier. Troops encountered blinding snows, winds too strong for the horses to face, temperatures that might fall to 40 degrees below zero and the danger of frostbite. At such times it was up to the officers to keep their men and animals moving at all costs, to find any sort of shelter until the worst was over and the trail could be resumed. (*Harper's Weekly*, January 28, 1888; R. F. Zogbaum.) OPPOSITE, TOP: An Army-courier relay station in Montana Territory in 1888. The Great Northern Reserve was a stretch of land about the size of the state of Maine along the Canadian border with the Missouri River as its southern boundary. Distances were so vast in this region that Army communications depended on a string of relay stations like this one where couriers could rest, get a meal and change horses. The Great Northern Reserve was occupied by over 10,000

Indians—Piegan, Gros Ventres and Northern Blackfoot. Farther south was the Crow reservation along the Yellowstone River. The Army's job in this region was to try to keep the peace between the Piegan and the Crow, who were traditional enemies, and the attempt to do so often led to skirmishing between the Cavalry and one tribe or the other. (*Harper's Weekly*, June 2, 1888.) OPPOSITE, BOTTOM: Reports of possible trouble on Cheyenne and Arapaho reservations brought Gen. Philip Sheridan (shown here seated on a rock as a local scout gives him some information) to the area around Fort Reno in 1885. Sheridan, hero of Cedar Creek in the Civil War, had already served against the Indians in the campaigns of 1868 and 1869. He was able to defuse this situation without major military action. (*Harper's Weekly*, August 8, 1885; R. F. Zogbaum.)

R.T. Zogbaum
'90

OPPOSITE: A party of Cheyenne scouts. As the Indian Wars
drew to a close, the practice of recruiting Indian scouts for the
Cavalry became more and more widespread. *Harper's* reported that
in 1888 the U.S. Army, which was then limited by law to 25,000
enlisted men, included 200 Indian scouts of different tribes. The
Indians received the same pay, uniforms and rations as regular
Army troops, plus about 40 cents a day extra if they furnished
their own horses. The leading Army commanders in the later
years of the Indian Wars, Miles, Crook and others, believed that
Indian scouts were essential, citing their work in the recently
completed campaign against Geronimo. (*Harper's Weekly*, May 25,
1889; R. F. Zogbaum.) ABOVE: A classic Remington illustration
of a Cavalry officer, published in 1889 under the title "The
Frontier Trooper's Thanatopsis." The skull lying on the plains in
front of the Indian burial structure has stimulated intense
contemplation of the meaning of life and death—*thanatos* being the
Greek word for death. (*Harper's Weekly*, April 13, 1889; Frederic
Remington.) RIGHT: A Cavalry officer of the period of the
campaign against Geronimo, Lt. Carter P. Johnson, sketched on
the frontier by Remington for *Harper's* in 1888. (*Harper's Weekly*,
December 22, 1888; Frederic Remington.)

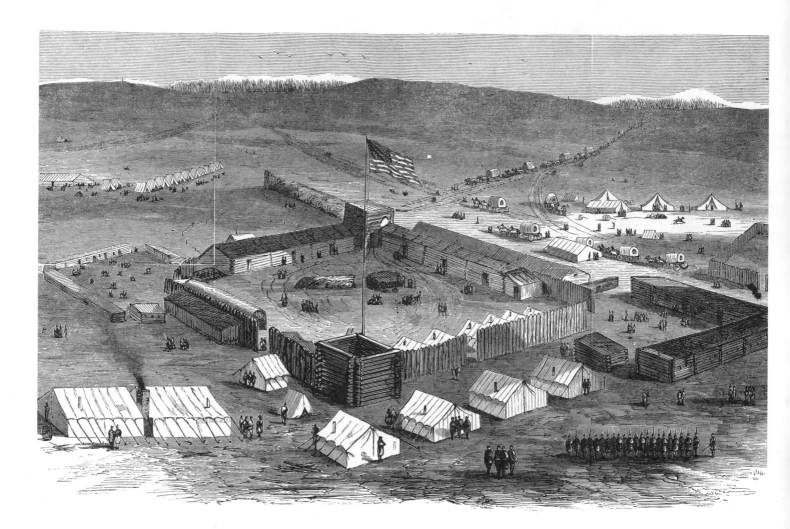

ABOVE: An excellent illustration of Camp Supply, Indian Territory, a frontier Army post during the Indian Wars. Located on the North Fork of the Canadian River, the fort was built, with walls ten feet high, in such a way that soldiers inside could cover any approach with rifle fire. (*Harper's Weekly*, February 27, 1869.)

OPPOSITE: This drawing of scouts leading a Cavalry troop was first published during a threatened Cheyenne outbreak in 1885. Indians often had a head start on the Cavalry, and the Cavalry officer's most demanding job was to track the enemy with the help of his scouts, catch up and still have men and horses in a condition to fight. Tracking was easiest in grassy country, and most difficult on hard, dry ground. Indians were adept at leaving false trails. In this picture, one of the scouts has found an old moccasin on the ground. Was it left behind in haste, or discarded to lead him off the trail? All of the scout's experience and knowledge came into play in deciphering the meaning of signs such as this. If he read them correctly, the superior Army horses could outperform the Indians'

ponies and make up for even a substantial head start. Even when dismounting just for a moment, the scout took his rifle with him. This was not only to have it in case of an ambush, but to be sure not to lose it should his horse be shot or startled and gallop off without him. (*Harper's Weekly*, August 1, 1885; T. de Thulstrup.)

OVERLEAF: An ambushed guard lies on the ground, killed on picket duty on the perimeter of the large camp seen in the background. The soldiers and the scout on the left hurry past the body, eager to pick up the trail of the enemy. More soldiers, having heard the shot, come up from the rear. If enough manpower was available, soldiers on picket duty around a Cavalry camp were checked on periodically during the night. Small squads like this one were kept ready with horses saddled to respond to shots or other signs of trouble. Experienced troopers felt the most dangerous hour was at first light, half an hour before sunrise. This was the Indian's favorite time to attack. (*Harper's Weekly*, May 29, 1886; T. de Thulstrup, from a sketch by Frederic Remington.)

OPPOSITE, TOP: Because soldiers on the frontier were paid only at long intervals, every two months under the best of conditions, it was necessary for the paymaster to carry substantial amounts of money when making the rounds of several posts and forts. Here a paymaster's stagecoach is being led through rugged and dangerous Southwestern terrain by heavily armed troopers proceeding cautiously on foot. (*Harper's Weekly*, June 4, 1887; R. F. Zogbaum.) OPPOSITE, BOTTOM: Soldiers of the Sixth Cavalry, stationed at Fort Bayard, New Mexico, in 1885. Here they are practicing a new drill, firing with carbines over their horses, which have been trained to lie down and remain still. It was felt that both horses and soldiers would provide smaller targets for enemy fire this way, and that the prone horses would give their riders some protection from enemy fire on the ground. It would take a few months to train the Army horses to lie down on command, usually a tap on their left legs, and to remain lying down while the battle raged around them. (*Harper's Weekly*, April 4, 1885; T. de Thulstrup, based on photographs by Ch. Barthelmess & Co.) ABOVE: Conducting military operations in the American desert brought its own problems. Here a Cavalry troop has been stopped in its tracks by an Arizona sandstorm. (*Harper's Weekly*, September 14, 1889; Frederic Remington.)

An Indian squaw mourning a slain warrior lying on a burial platform. This illustration was published by *Harper's* a few weeks after the Wounded Knee Massacre under the title "The Last Scene of the Last Act of the Sioux War." Artist H. F. Farny's original title had simply been "The Last Vigil." (*Harper's Weekly*, February 14, 1891; H. F. Farny.)

Scenes from the Indian Wars

WARFARE AGAINST THE Indians followed settlers to every area of the American West in the second half of the nineteenth century. As the Oregon Trail brought the first wagon trains to the Pacific Northwest after 1840, that area saw some violent clashes between local Indians and these first settlers. After the Rogue River War (1855–56), most of the Indians in northern California and southern Oregon agreed to live on reservations. The Army was less successful farther north. The Yakima War in the mid-1850s against Indians who were on the warpath from Seattle to the Walla Walla Valley ended inconclusively. A further expedition later in the decade succeeded in making the Washington settlements more secure.

In the Southwest, American occupation of New Mexico Territory in 1846 began a war against the Navajo and the Apache that continued, off and on, for 40 years. Before the Civil War, settlements there were sparse. Still, perhaps 200 to 300 settlers were killed in sporadic raids in the 1850s. The Army undertook a number of offensives in reply but had success only against the Jicarilla Apache in 1854 and the Utes in 1855. Action heated up in 1860, and by 1865 the Navajo had surrendered and settled on a reservation along New Mexico's Pecos River. The Apache accepted life on the reservation for a time, but by 1872 were on the warpath again. On December 26, 1872, at Salt River and at Turret Butte, in the south-central part of present-day Arizona, Col. George Crook won important victories. The following year the Apache returned to the reservation. After a decade of relative calm, the mid-1880s saw the last Apache uprising. Geronimo's final surrender in 1886 to Gen. Nelson A. Miles, Crook's successor, ended the Apache wars.

The long history, alternating between treaties and warfare, of the federal government's relations with the Sioux and other tribes on the northern plains illustrates everything that went wrong with American Indian policy during the nineteenth century. By the middle of the century it was obvious in Washington that settlers in increasing numbers, miners, even railroad builders, would one day push far beyond the Mississippi onto the Plains Indians' traditional lands. Hoping to prevent trouble, the government negotiated the First Treaty of Fort Laramie in 1851 with the Sioux, Shoshoni, Cheyenne and Arapaho. The treaty assigned specific reservations to each tribe as well as providing for financial annuities for the Indians. Events soon shattered any hope for permanent peace. The Minnesota Sioux were dissatisfied with their treaty and the failure of the government to live up to its obligations under it. They went on a bloody uprising in 1862. This uprising was ruthlessly suppressed after about 400 settlers had been killed. Two years later, while this situation was still smoldering, a disaster occurred that had far-reaching implications.

On November 29, 1864, at Sand Creek in the southeastern part of the Colorado territory, a militia force of about 1,000 Colorado volunteers led by Col. John M. Chivington attacked a Cheyenne and Arapaho camp. The militia under the fanatical Chivington were reacting to the killing of an emigrant party near Denver that winter. These Cheyenne, however, led by Chief Black Kettle, were not responsible for the atrocity, and had been negotiating for peace. They had located their camp with the permission of the commander of a local Army fort, and a number of their warriors were away negotiating a peace treaty with the government when the massacre occurred. Even as the surprise attack began, Black Kettle tried to prevent it, raising both a white and an American flag. The attack continued despite these efforts. About 300 Indians were killed, more than two-thirds of them women and children. This treacherous and cowardly assault was never forgotten by the Plains Indians. Black Kettle himself survived Sand Creek. Four years later he was killed by Custer's troops at the Battle of Washita in the Indian Territory just east of the Texas Panhandle.

Having forfeited any hope of immediate peace with the Cheyenne and Arapaho, the government next managed to lose the Sioux by beginning to build and fortify a road from Fort Laramie, in present-day Wyoming, to the Montana gold fields. The road, known either as the Bozeman Trail or the Powder River Road, crossed favorite Sioux hunting grounds in the Bighorn Mountains. The result was 16,000 Sioux warriors on the warpath under the leadership of Chief Red Cloud. Workers at various military outposts along the route came under steady attack. This culminated in the Fetterman Massacre of December 21, 1866, when 80 soldiers were killed near Fort Phil Kearney. In the face of Red Cloud's relentless opposition, the government finally agreed to abandon the Bozeman Trail, and the forts along it, including Fort Phil Kearney. When the soldiers left, the Indians burned the forts to the ground. The settlement was formalized in the 1868 Second Treaty of Fort Laramie whereby the Sioux were granted possession of all of South Dakota west of the Missouri River. Having made his point, Red Cloud agreed to settle on a Nebraska reservation. A considerable statesman, Red Cloud continued to criticize the policies of the government. He even made several trips to Washington in his later years to argue the Indians' cause. He died in his eighties in 1909.

With some good will on both sides, the Second Treaty of Fort Laramie might have provided a lasting framework for peace with the Sioux. An unforeseeable event, however, destroyed any hope for peace. In the mid-1870s gold was discovered in South Dakota's Black Hills and thousands of prospectors overran the Sioux lands. This precipitated the next round of warfare, including the most famous battle of the Indian Wars, the Custer massacre of June 25, 1876.

There were three major Army columns in the Sioux country of Montana in late June 1876. While the column led by Gen. George Crook was stalled on the Rosebud River, the two others, commanded by Gen. Alfred Terry and Col. John Gibbon, planned to link up on the Little Bighorn River on June 26. Custer, taking 600 troops of the Seventh Cavalry detached from Terry's column to make a forward reconnaissance, covered 83 miles in 24 hours. When he reached the river, Custer, unaware that there were at least 3,000 Sioux and Cheyenne warriors in the immediate area under Sitting Bull, Crazy Horse and Gall, divided his forces into three groups to patrol different areas. Custer's group of 210 were wiped out completely in less than an hour. Fifty-three more soldiers were killed in a subsidiary battle four miles away. Five more died in the next few months of wounds received that day. The total of 268 killed as a result of the Little Bighorn made it the worst defeat in the history of the Indian Wars.

From a more distant perspective, however, the Custer debacle was just an incident in a larger campaign. Terry trapped 3,000 Sioux later that summer at the Tongue River Valley. Sitting Bull fled to Canada, and the Sioux surrendered on October 31, after which most returned to the Dakota reservation. Sitting Bull eventually returned from Canada and he too accepted the reservation. The Wounded Knee Massacre, on December 29, 1890, was the last armed encounter between the U.S. military and the Sioux. After the bodies were buried at Wounded Knee, the Indian Wars were over.

ABOVE: Indians of an unidentified tribe deciding the fate of a prisoner. This drawing is by Felix O. C. Darley, the most prominent American book illustrator of the mid-nineteenth century. The prolific Darley illustrated the works of Washington Irving, James Fenimore Cooper and a score of other standard American authors during his long career. He had, however, also traveled on the plains beyond the Mississippi River as a young man in the 1840s. He created from firsthand experience scenes of buffalo hunting and wagon trains heading West. Reproduced by lithography, these illustrations hung on the walls of tens of thousands of American homes in the middle years of the century. When this illustration was published in 1860, the Plains Indians were already ravaged by smallpox and other diseases, and were facing the decline of the great buffalo herds even before the final, most destructive era of buffalo hunting had begun. Many in the East felt the Indians would soon simply pass into history. This view, echoed in the article that accompanied this picture, hardly predicted the three decades of hard-fought armed conflict that would soon begin with the Sioux uprising of 1862. (*The Illustrated London News*, January 28, 1860; Felix O. C. Darley.) OPPOSITE, TOP: A scene that must have replayed itself many times in the minds of those who decided, after passage of the Homestead Act of 1862, to try farming on the Western plains. This illustration shows Sioux warriors, well-armed with both rifles and bows and arrows, creeping up on a farmer plowing his field. (*Harper's Weekly*, May 2, 1868; W. M. Cary.) OPPOSITE, BOTTOM: The interior of a settler's cabin during an Indian raid. (*Harper's Weekly*, July 16, 1870; C. S. Reinhart.)

174   *Scenes from the Indian Wars*

OPPOSITE, TOP: A family of settlers murdered by the Sioux during the 1862 Minnesota uprising. During the 1850s the Santee Sioux agreed to live on a Minnesota reservation. Dissatisfaction with the treaties they had signed, the continuing encroachment of settlers and the failure of the government to deliver annuities they had pledged resulted in the 1862 uprising, led by Chief Little Crow, along the Minnesota River. In late August 1862, New Ulm and other settlements were devastated and over 400 settlers were killed. The Army regrouped and struck back, defeating the Sioux decisively at Wood Lake on September 23. (*Frank Leslie's Illustrated Newspaper*, October 25, 1862.) OPPOSITE, BOTTOM: The Indians who surrendered were tried, and over 200 Sioux warriors were sentenced to death. President Lincoln commuted the sentences of all but 38, who were hanged at Mankato, Minnesota, on December 26, 1862. This was the largest mass execution in American history. This illustration of the Mankato execution was based on a sketch by an eyewitness. The blindfolded Indians were all hanged simultaneously. It was reported that one of the ropes broke as soon as the scaffold was released. The unfortunate victim was immediately strung up again. (*Frank Leslie's Illustrated Newspaper*, January 24, 1863; based on a sketch by W. H. Childs.) ABOVE: Sioux warriors and the Cavalry battling outside Fort Phil Kearney

during the long conflict over the government's attempt to open up and guard the Bozeman Trail. In this battle, which is often called the Fetterman Massacre after one of the officers killed, a band of Sioux under Chief High Backbone trapped and killed more than 80 soldiers outside the fort on December 21, 1866. Many Western forts were small, but Fort Phil Kearney, despite its isolated location on the upper Powder River, had 30 buildings contained within a 2,800-foot-long wooden stockade. Such comparative grandeur did not come cheaply on the frontier. More than a hundred military and civilian workers were killed hauling timber to the fort during its construction, and in some circles it earned the nickname Fort Perilous. The building of the fort proved to be an exercise in futility impressive even by Army standards. After heavy losses incurred building and defending it, in 1868 the government agreed to abandon both the fort and the Bozeman Trail by the Second Treaty of Fort Laramie, which created a huge Sioux reservation centered in South Dakota's Black Hills. Later that year, after the Army left, Chief Red Cloud's braves burned Fort Phil Kearney to the ground. It lasted such a short time that it is difficult to find a Western map on which it appears. (*Harper's Weekly*, March 23, 1867.)

OPPOSITE, TOP: Artist Theodore R. Davis was with these troops in Kansas in the summer of 1867 when they discovered the remains of Lt. L. S. Kidder and ten Seventh Cavalry soldiers who had been traveling from Fort Sedgwick, in present-day northeastern Colorado, with orders for Custer from Gen. Sherman. Kidder's detachment had been completely wiped out by the Sioux. None of the remains could be individually identified, and they were immediately buried on the spot where they were found. (*Harper's Weekly*, August 17, 1867; Theodore R. Davis.) OPPOSITE, BOTTOM: A party of scouts fighting off a stampede of horses started by the Sioux outside Fort Union on the Yellowstone River in the Dakota Territory. Even the smaller Western forts were difficult for the Indians to attack directly, but herds of horses and other animals kept outside the walls were vulnerable to raiding parties throughout the Indian Wars. The stands being used to steady their rifles by the men firing in the foreground are a feature not often seen in illustrations on this theme. Artist W. M. Cary had witnessed such a scene at Fort Union some years before this illustration was published. (*Frank Leslie's Illustrated Newspaper*, May 30, 1868; W. M. Cary.) RIGHT: A portrait of Sitting Bull, Teton Dakota Indian chief. He was the dominant figure in the final phase of the Indian Wars on the northern plains. This illustration was published just before Sitting Bull was killed during the events that led up to the Wounded Knee Massacre. (*The Illustrated London News*, December 13, 1890.) BELOW: A prisoner, staked to the plains, guarded by a single Indian with a rifle. This is one of the many striking images of Indian life painted by Henry F. Farny in the last decades of the nineteenth century. Farny was born in France, which his family was forced to leave for political reasons in the 1850s. He grew up in western Pennsylvania and Cincinnati, where he later maintained his studio. Working as an illustrator of, among other things, the McGuffey readers, Farny decided to concentrate on Indian life. He traveled extensively through the Indian country on the northern plains in the early 1880s, absorbing the atmosphere and collecting artifacts. Historian Robert Taft has pointed out that the presence of trousers on this prisoner may owe more to Victorian propriety and Farny's interest in getting his picture exhibited—he originally painted it in watercolor—than to the actual history of the treatment of prisoners by the Plains Indians. (*Harper's Weekly*, February 13, 1886; H. F. Farny.)

OPPOSITE: Indians at the Standing Rock Agency in the Dakota Territory in 1883. Sitting Bull had fled across the Canadian border after the Little Bighorn, but within a few years, with his people starving, he had no choice but to surrender to the American military. He did so at Fort Buford, northern Dakota Territory, in July 1881. He was eventually settled at the Standing Rock Agency where he lived throughout most of the 1880s. He occasionally left the Agency to tour with Buffalo Bill's Wild West show by permission of Indian agents who wanted him out of the way while they purchased tribal lands—something to which Sitting Bull was always opposed. Farny's illustration shows a typical ration day (the day food was distributed) at Standing Rock in the 1880s. (*Harper's Weekly*, July 28, 1883; H. F. Farny.) ABOVE: An Indian census being taken at a reservation near Bismarck in the Dakota Territory in 1886. The Indian standing in the center of the front row with one hand resting on the table is Chief Gall, one of the legendary Sioux warriors and victor, with Sitting Bull and Crazy Horse, over Custer at the Little Bighorn in 1876. (*Frank Leslie's Illustrated Newspaper*, November 20, 1886; based on a photograph by D. F. Barry.)

The Sioux ghost dance. *Frank Leslie's* claimed this illustration had been drawn by "D. Smith from sketches made on the spot." It is unclear, however, whether illustrator Dan Smith was actually the one on the spot who made the sketches. The ghost-dance movement, fascinating in itself, is memorable because it precipitated the Wounded Knee Massacre of December 29, 1890. Belief in the ghost dance began among the Paiutes of Nevada around 1870, and spread during the 1880s to the Arapaho, Northern Cheyenne and the Oglala Sioux. It was a movement based on a longing to return to the past. It promised that dead ancestors and the legendary buffalo herds would be restored to life, and that an Indian messiah would come who would sweep away the white man. The ghost dance was actively embraced by the Sioux on South Dakota's Pine Ridge Reservation, who in 1890 were suffering through the first part of a difficult winter. They were cold, hungry and ravaged by disease. Sitting Bull was then living at Pine Ridge, and was a strong advocate of the ghost dance.

Believing that he might instigate unrest, the authorities decided to arrest him. On December 15, 1890, reservation police battled with Sitting Bull's supporters over the arrest, a battle in which Sitting Bull and several policemen were killed. Fearing reprisals for these deaths, another Sioux chief, Big Foot, immediately led a band of about 350 of his people off the reservation toward one of their old camps on the Cheyenne River. Big Foot and his followers were intercepted by the Cavalry, who led them instead to a camp on Wounded Knee Creek. The final battle broke out when a force of about 500 soldiers demanded the Indians' weapons, and then, supported by cannon, opened fire when a struggle started over a young brave's rifle. Big Foot was among the 153 Indians killed, at least 60 of whom were women and children. About 30 soldiers were also killed. Many of the victims were buried in a mass grave the following spring after the frozen ground had thawed. (*Frank Leslie's Illustrated Newspaper*, January 10, 1891; Dan Smith.)

ABOVE: The immediate aftermath of Wounded Knee was some subsidiary incidents in the vicinity of the massacre. *Frank Leslie's* reported that on January 5, 1891, a wagon train was attacked between Rapid City and Wounded Knee by a band of about 100 Indians. They were held off by the teamsters, as illustrated here, for six hours until the Cavalry, then stretched very thin over a large area, could arrive. (*Frank Leslie's Illustrated Newspaper*, January 17, 1891; Dan Smith.) RIGHT: R. Caton Woodville of *The Illustrated London News* was at Pine Ridge at the time of Wounded Knee and sketched these two braves during the aftermath when major violence was feared by the military. The ubiquitous Gen. Nelson A. Miles took control of the situation, however, and peace was restored. (*The Illustrated London News*, January 17, 1891; R. Caton Woodville.)

ABOVE: This fanciful interpretation of the Battle of Washita shows Custer, on horseback at left, leading his Seventh Cavalry troops into the winter quarters of Black Kettle's Cheyenne on the Washita River at dawn on November 27, 1868. On the evening before the surprise attack, Black Kettle had returned from a meeting some days before with Gen. William B. Hazen at Fort Cobb, 100 miles down the Washita Valley. Hazen had refused to allow the Cheyenne leader to bring his people to the fort for the winter. He had sent Black Kettle away with the assurance, which proved worthless, that the Cheyenne would not be attacked if they kept the peace themselves. As Custer's troops attacked the village, Black Kettle rode out to attempt to make peace; he was shot off his horse and trampled by the Cavalry before he had a chance to ask for the meeting. The Cheyenne were totally routed at Washita. More than 100 Indians were killed, including women and children, and 875 captured horses were put to death by Custer and his soldiers, who also burned the Cheyenne village and all it contained. As neighboring Arapaho, Kiowa and Comanche braves started to come to the Cheyenne's rescue, Custer marched 53 women and children prisoners back to his base at Camp Supply on the North Canadian River, 60 miles to the north, where they were met by a triumphant Gen. Sheridan. Custer did lose a platoon of 16 men who were killed by a band of Arapaho from a neighboring village. Sheridan subsequently tried to justify the Washita mas-

sacre. In an outright lie, he claimed that Black Kettle had refused to bring his people to the fort for sanctuary. Washita was one of the beginnings of the end for the southern Plains Indians. The superior weaponry of the Cavalry and new battle techniques, such as the winter attack, began to take a heavy toll. (*Frank Leslie's Illustrated Newspaper*, December 26, 1868.) OPPOSITE, TOP: An incident from the history of the Northern Cheyenne that took place years after they were settled on their Montana reservation south of the Yellowstone River. Two young Cheyenne braves had murdered a white man and were being tracked in the hills by the local Cavalry. Tired of hiding, they sent word challenging the Army to an open fight for their lives, threatening further crimes if they were not obliged. The two Indians, descendants of the great Cheyenne warriors of earlier years, were duly killed after an all-out assault on the soldiers. Artist Walter Shirlaw was there to sketch the drama as an eyewitness. (*Harper's Weekly*, October 18, 1890; Walter Shirlaw.) OPPOSITE, BOTTOM: Indians on the Cheyenne and Arapaho reservation in present-day Oklahoma killing cattle that had been issued to them by the government. With the buffalo long gone, the government undertook at times to supply cattle to Indians on various reservations. This was one of the factors that promoted the great expansion of the cattle industry north of Texas after 1870. (*Harper's Weekly*, January 4, 1890; R. F. Zogbaum.)

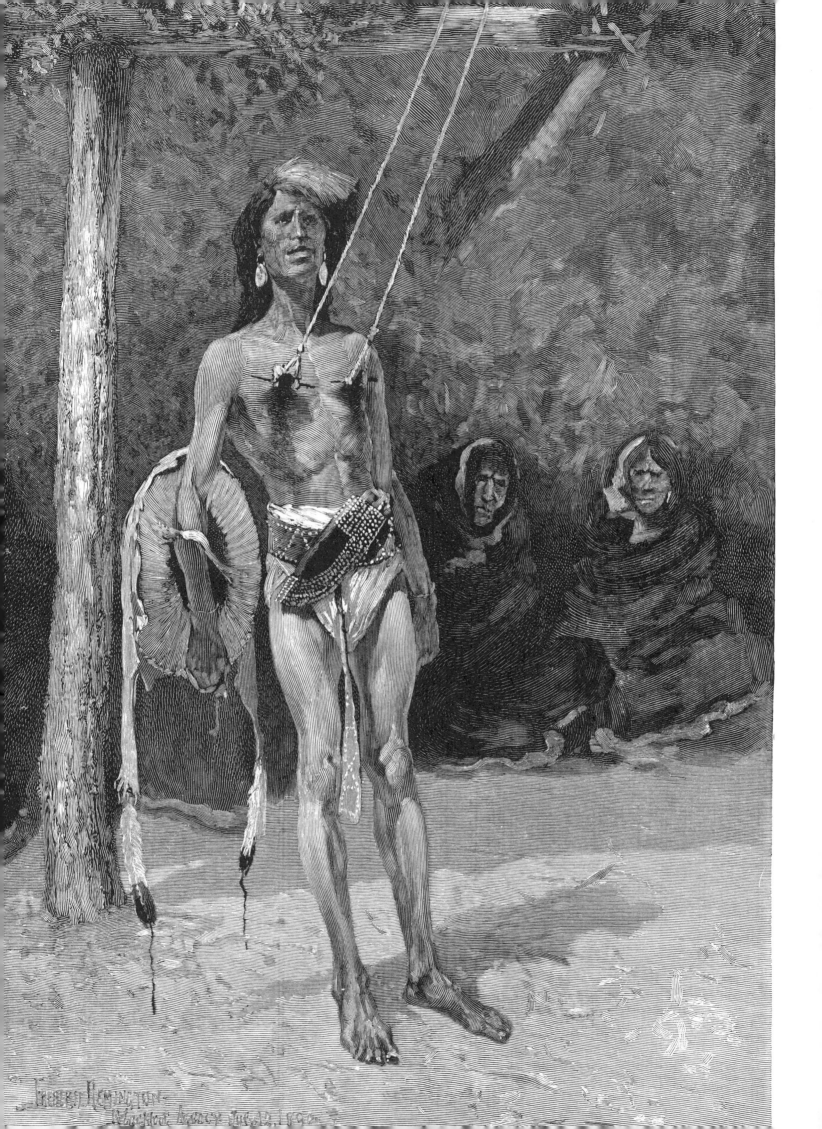

OPPOSITE: A classic Remington illustration of a Blackfoot Indian undergoing the rigors of the sun dance. This was the principal tribal religious ceremony, and was held each summer. When successfully completed, it marked the worthy young Indian's acceptance by the men of his tribe as a full-fledged warrior. After a period of fasting, the young man preparing for this ordeal had four incisions made in his chest by the tribal medicine man. Short wooden sticks were then inserted between each pair of incisions, and rawhide ropes from a central pole were attached to the ends of the sticks. With his weight on the ropes, the young brave would hang suspended, sometimes facing the sun in an attitude of supplication, at other times dancing, singing or reciting stories of past and future bravery, until the sticks tore through his flesh and released him. The sun-dance ritual could go on for three or four days. The ceremony was also practiced among the Arapaho, Cheyenne, Sioux and other tribes. (*Harper's Weekly*, December 13, 1890; Frederic Remington.) ABOVE: An incident from the wars of the 1870s. *Harper's* reported that when a group of Piegans wanted to sue for peace in 1870, they brought the head of a famous killer of white settlers to Gen. De Trobriand to prove their sincerity. When the general received this unusual offering it was noted that the dead man had been ravaged by smallpox, which was then rampant among the Blackfoot tribes. (*Harper's Weekly*, April 30, 1870; W. M. Cary.)

OPPOSITE: A scene from the Nez Percé campaign of 1877. The illustration shows some of the 5,000 troops under Gen. O. O. Howard who tracked the Nez Percé leader, Chief Joseph, and his band of about 250 warriors for five months and 1,000 miles through parts of Idaho, Montana and Yellowstone Park. The Indians, recognizing the inevitable, surrendered on October 5 after being besieged by Gen. Nelson A. Miles 30 miles short of the Canadian border across which they had hoped to escape. During the long campaign the Nez Percé inflicted heavy casualties on the Army, including 266 troopers killed. The Idaho scene in this illustration, based on a sketch by an Army officer, was no doubt aptly named the "Dead Mule Trail." The story of the Nez Percé is typical of what happened to many Indian peoples in the nineteenth century. They were originally based in what is now central Idaho and areas of present-day Washington and Oregon. Their name is French for "pierced nose," though by the nineteenth century the practice of wearing nose pendants seems to have been largely abandoned. They lived off the abundant salmon in small villages along the rivers. After acquiring the horse early in the eighteenth century, they became more warlike and adopted many of the customs of the Plains Indians, who lived east of their traditional lands. The Nez Percé became expert horsemen, developing a huge herd and practicing some breeding techniques. In the mid-1850s a treaty with the U.S. government made most of their traditional lands into a reservation. Chances for permanent peace were lost, however, when gold was found on the Salmon and other rivers in 1860, and miners overran the area. The federal government attempted to push through a new treaty reducing the reservation

to a quarter of its original size, thereby clearing much of the land for the prospectors. The Nez Percé refused to accept this scheme, and the 1877 war was the eventual result. After his long and brilliant campaign, Chief Joseph surrendered when he realized, with winter coming on, that his people would die of cold and starvation while besieged by federal troops. At the time of his surrender he issued his famous valedictory to his warriors, "I am tired of fighting. My heart is sick and sad. From where the sun now stands I will fight no more forever." Chief Joseph was then 37 years old. (*Harper's Weekly*, September 29, 1877.) BELOW: The captured Nez Percé amusing themselves in their temporary village near Fort Leavenworth, Kansas, early in 1878. Those captured were eventually assigned to a reservation in the Indian Territory, and were not allowed to rejoin their people in the Northwest as the government had promised. (*Frank Leslie's Illustrated Newspaper*, February 23, 1878; F. J. Howell.) BELOW, INSET: Chief Joseph of the Nez Percé. (*Harper's Weekly*, August 18, 1877; Vincent Colyer.) OVERLEAF: The Indian Wars on the northern plains were winding down when Remington published this illustration of an incident on the Montana Crow reservation in 1887. It involved an armed confrontation between a band of Indians and government agents. Traditional enemies of the Blackfoot and Dakota tribes, the Crow had often sided with the whites against other tribes of Plains Indians in the wars of the 1860s and 1870s. They were rewarded in 1868 by being given a reservation on their traditional lands in Montana. (*Harper's Weekly*, November 5, 1887; Frederic Remington.)

ABOVE: A scene from the 1879 Ute War in Colorado, a company of Ninth Cavalry black troops coming to the aid of fellow soldiers besieged by Indians for several days. The Utes inhabited western Colorado and eastern Utah (the name Utah is derived from their name). They acquired horses only in the first part of the nineteenth century, later than some other Indian groups. They then became habitual predators on the livestock owned by white settlers in their region. Defeat in a long war (1864–70) left them on a reservation in southwestern Colorado. Their refusal to remain there, and continued raids on nearby settlers, game and livestock, led to the incident pictured here. The beleaguered federal troops were relieved by a large force of Cavalry in addition to this black company, which just happened to be in the area. The Utes were again subdued, although the Indian Agency buildings had been burned and the Indian agent for the Utes murdered in this conflict. The episode is sometimes referred to as the Meeker Massacre, named after the murdered Indian agent. (*Harper's*

Weekly, November 1, 1879; C. S. Reinhart.) OPPOSITE, TOP: Eight years after the Meeker Massacre, the Utes, who had been transferred from Colorado to a reservation in Utah, were again in conflict with the local and federal governments. Preferring the hunting lands around their former reservation, a small band led by a chief named Colorow returned to Colorado and remained there for several years in violation of government policy. Eventually conflict with local settlers broke out again. A band of Utes numbering about 200, well armed with Winchester repeating rifles and plentiful ammunition, followed Colorow into the back country. They were pursued by a force comprised of some local sheriffs and their deputies, some volunteer local cowboys and about 200 state militia. This illustration shows some settlers leaving their isolated cabin for the relative security of a nearby town after having seen an Indian signal fire. (*Frank Leslie's Illustrated Newspaper*, September 3, 1887.)

RIGHT: On the same day as the illustration above was published by *Frank Leslie's*, *Harper's* released this drawing of the pursuers of Colorow and the rugged terrain on which they would have to fight. It is virtually certain that *Harper's* artist Charles Graham was not on the scene at the time, but he did know the territory from previous trips. Front-page news was commonly reported in the nation's illustrated press in this casual way at that time. Colorow's band was eventually subdued. (*Harper's Weekly*, September 3, 1887; Charles Graham.)

ABOVE: Modoc Indians in their stronghold in the lava beds near Tule Lake in northern California during the Modoc War of 1873. Unhappy on an Oregon reservation, about 75 Modoc warriors and their families, after some violent skirmishes with the local white population, retreated to the lava beds, an area of ravines, caves, unusual rock formations and fissures they knew well. In January 1873 Gen. Edward Canby attacked with 400 soldiers of the First Cavalry and Twenty-First Infantry regiments. He was repulsed by the Modocs, who killed 16 soldiers and wounded 53. (*Harper's Weekly*, May 3, 1873.) OPPOSITE, BOTTOM: The climactic event of the Modoc War: the murder of General Canby by the Modoc chief known to history as Captain Jack, on April 11, 1873, during a meeting to see if peace could be arranged. The Modocs had murdered a number of white settlers on their way to the lava beds. Thus Canby was unable to agree to Captain Jack's demand that the government should withdraw and allow his people to remain in the lava beds unmolested. Unwilling to turn any of his people over to the Army, Captain Jack drew a concealed revolver and killed Canby. On April 15–17 a concentrated mortar attack drove

the Modocs from their stronghold. They were gradually captured a few at a time after having held off 1,000 soldiers and settlers for months. Captain Jack was captured on June 1, tried at Fort Klamath and hanged along with three of his followers on October 3, 1873. It was reported that workmen were busy building the gallows while the trial was going on. It had cost the Army 83 dead and 98 wounded soldiers, and half a million dollars, to round up less than a hundred Modoc warriors, who altogether lost 14 killed, four hanged and one suicide. The remaining Modocs were sent to the Indian Territory. When the tribe was allowed to return to Oregon in 1909, only 51 Modocs survived. Captain Jack's career did not end with his execution. Some frontier entrepreneur smuggled his body out of Fort Klamath and had it embalmed, after which the corpse of the Modoc chief toured the Eastern states as a sideshow attraction. The ratio of casualties suffered by the Army to the number of enemy warriors involved made the fight against the Modocs the costliest Indian campaign since the Seminole Wars of the 1830s. (*The Illustrated London News*, May 31, 1873; Arthur Hopkins, based on sketches by William Simpson.)

LEFT: The frustration the Army encountered in trying to dislodge the Modocs from the lava beds made the war a big story in the East. This illustration of a Modoc scalping party was published while the fighting was still going on. (*Harper's Weekly*, May 17, 1873.)

194 *Scenes from the Indian Wars*

OPPOSITE, TOP: An Apache poised to ambush a wagon in Arizona's Sierra Madre Mountains. The long, intermittent war against the Apaches of Arizona began in the 1860s with conflicts between early settlers and small contingents of federal troops on one side and the Apaches led by the great warriors Cochise and Mangas Coloradas on the other. During the Civil War, Arizona's Apaches were largely unchecked, but military opposition to them increased after the war ended. Still, Cochise and about 200 of his followers eluded the Army until September 1871, when they surrendered to Gen. George Crook, who had been successful in bringing other Apaches onto the reservation. Cochise escaped early in 1872, but later surrendered again, and died in 1874. (*Harper's Magazine*, May 1891; Frederic Remington.) OPPOSITE, BOTTOM: The Apache Wars were reaching their climax when Remington published this illustration in *Harper's* early in 1886. The mounted rider arriving at an Arizona ranch is warning of an impending attack. Later that year the artist would travel to Arizona to cover the military campaign against Geronimo. Remington did not travel with the soldiers who tracked the Apache leader that year across hundreds of miles of Arizona's inaccessible terrain, but he did become familiar with the area, and returned often in later years to the theme of the final struggles of Geronimo. (*Harper's Weekly*, January 30, 1886; Frederic Remington.) ABOVE: Geronimo (right) and his fellow Apache Natchez in a wood engraving made from a photograph. The scene follows their final surrender on September 3, 1886, the event that marked the end of the Indian Wars in the Southwest. At the time of his surrender Geronimo was almost 60 years old. He had been fighting for the freedom and independence of his people, the Chiricahua Apaches, for almost 40 years. He first fought the Mexicans, who in 1858 had been responsible for the death of his wife and children. In 1874 the U.S. authorities forced 4,000

Apaches onto a reservation at San Carlos in east-central Arizona, an area that has been described as a barren wasteland. Deprived of their rights and often hungry, Geronimo and other militant leaders led the Apaches on a campaign of bloodshed and revenge. Peace was established by the then Lt. Col. Crook in the mid-1870s, but his successors in the Department of Arizona were unable to maintain it after Geronimo and his followers once again fled the reservation. Crook was recalled in September 1882. Fifteen months later Geronimo was back on the reservation, only to leave again with a small band of followers—fewer than 150 men, women and children—in May 1885. By this time the American authorities were desperate to end the struggle against Geronimo permanently. In March 1886 Geronimo and his followers surrendered again, this time at the Cañón de los Embudos in Sonora, Mexico, but fled after hearing rumors that they would be murdered once back in the United States. The following month Crook was replaced by Gen. Nelson A. Miles. Miles's soldiers tracked Geronimo for five months over 1,600 miles and finally induced him to surrender for the last time on September 3, 1886, at Skeleton Canyon, Arizona. Miles promised Geronimo that after an indefinite period he and his people would be allowed to settle in Arizona, but the government failed to keep that promise. Instead, they transported Geronimo and 450 others to Florida, where they were held on an Army base. In 1894 Geronimo was moved to Fort Sill, Oklahoma. He was allowed considerable freedom: he appeared at the Louisiana Purchase Exposition in 1904, where he reportedly did a lively business in Geronimo souvenirs, and rode in Theodore Roosevelt's inaugural parade the following year. However, he never saw Arizona again. He died at Fort Sill in 1909 at the age of 79. (*Harper's Weekly*, October 2, 1886; from a photograph by A. Frank Randall.)

The campaign against Geronimo was over when Remington published this illustration under the title "Geronimo and His Band Returning from a Raid into Mexico" in 1888. In 1913, four years after Geronimo's death, the Apaches being held in Oklahoma were given the choice of settling there permanently or moving to the Mescalero Reservation in New Mexico—about two-thirds chose New Mexico. (*Harper's Weekly*, August 18, 1888; Frederic Remington.)

General Index

Index of Artists